My Mother Is Now Earth

My Mother Is Now Earth

Mark Anthony Rolo

BOREALIS BOOKS

ACKNOWLEDGMENTS

Melanie Dylan Fox, Pamela Herron Stover, Bao Phi, Andrea Potter, Judy Adrian, Christina Rencontre, Diana Lee King, Nita Osborn, Aurora Powers, Laura Baker, and Peter Oresick.

A very special thanks to my dear friend and editor, Ann Regan, for understanding and supporting this story from the beginning.

My mother would only be honored.

Borealis Books is an imprint of the Minnesota Historical Society Press. www.mhspress.org

The Minnesota Historical Society Press is a member of the Association of American University Presses.

Manufactured in the United States of America

10 9 8 7 6 5 4 3 2 1

♾ The paper used in this publication meets the minimum requirements of the American National Standard for Information Sciences—Permanence for Printed Library Materials, ANSI Z39.48–1984.

International Standard Book Number
ISBN: 978-0-87351-853-6 (cloth)
ISBN: 978-0-87351-859-8 (e-book)

Library of Congress Cataloging-in-Publication Data
Rolo, Mark Anthony.
My mother is now Earth / Mark Anthony Rolo.
p. cm.
ISBN 978-0-87351-853-6 (cloth : alk. paper)—
ISBN 978-0-087351-859-8 (e-book)
1. Rolo. Mark Anthony—Family. 2. Rolo, Mark Anthony—Childhood and youth.
3. Ojibwa Indians—Ethnic identity. 4. Rolo, Corrine Winifred Bennett, 1926–1973.
5. Ojibwa women—Minnesota—Big Falls—Biography. 6. Ojibwa Indians—
Minnesota—Big Falls—Biography. 7. Mothers and sons. 8. Mothers—Death—
Psychological aspects. 9. Dreams—Psychological aspects. 10. Big Falls (Minn.)—
Biography. I. Title
E99.C6R728 2012
305.897′333077679—dc23
2011041158

To my nephew

NICHOLAS BRENNAN ROLO

CONTENTS

PROLOGUE

December 21, 2010

I have not dreamed about my mother in over thirty-five years. But last night I saw her. She was standing near the kitchen sink of the old burnt-out farmhouse of my boyhood in northern Minnesota. She wore her green dress, stained with grease and speckled with flour dust. I watched as she unfolded a gray hand towel and covered her bowl of bread dough. My mother sighed, wiped her brown forehead, and pulled back strands of black hair. Leaning against the sink, she stared into her yellow plastic cup of cold coffee, then asked what I had been up to all of these years. I shrugged and told her, "Not much, just teaching and some writing on the side." I said nothing about working on this book, nothing about the first rough pages I had just completed. She raised the cup to her lips and smiled. I felt it was time to leave and reached behind her to place an empty glass I was holding in the sink. Ever so lightly, I touched her warm, bare arm with my own. Suddenly she turned into glass and fell to the floor. I looked down and saw shards of my mother glistening like snow crystals under a bright morning sun. I looked into her glaring eyes and heard her soft but stern voice. "You need to be more careful."

⟫[1971]⟪

ᐳ[1]ᐸ

The Story of Snakes

My mother wants to be buried in fire.

She races into a burning farmhouse, letting serpent flames twist around her legs. She stumbles in the black haze, straddles the edge of a fiery grave, waiting to be tripped into the Earth.

My father leaps across the snows between the barn and the house. He pushes his way through the thick, dark smoke, reaching out, trying to touch her.

He finds her through her screams—"My babies! My babies!" My father pries her fingers from flaming beams and snatches her away from crumbling walls.

He drags my mother to snow, smothering her fire legs, wiping away her lava tears, raising his voice above hers.

"Goddamn it, Corrine! Listen to me! The babies are safe!"

And they are. My older brother Dennis is hiding with the babies in a woodshed out back.

"Was I one of the babies in that woodshed?"

"Keep your voice down," Dennis whispers, pushing his cold hand against my mouth. "She can hear you."

"Well, was I or not?"

"I'll finish telling you later."

"Just tell me that much."

"No. You weren't even born yet."

I wait until the roar of the Oldsmobile rises, then I ask Dennis about our mother's snake scars. "She got those from that fire, didn't she?"

He stares out the window and says no.

I can see only the silver top of the U-Haul trailer from where I sit on the floor of my father's Oldsmobile. I lean my head against the back of the seat, behind my mother. She holds my baby brother in her arms. I can hear his slurping. I can feel her soft breathing.

When we left Milwaukee this morning, it was still dark and the winter was almost melted away. But the closer we get to Minnesota, each time my father pulls over to get gas in a new town, the fatter the snow becomes.

We are going back in time.

Before, my mother packed her baking pans in cardboard boxes and got after us six kids to stuff our clothes into paper bags. My father never said much about where he was moving us to—Big Falls.

"They got a grocery and hardware store, a post office. You kids will be catching a school bus. It goes right past the farm."

Once we cross the river into Minnesota, the night fills the Oldsmobile. I can smell my father's rolled cigarette. I can hear him trying to make my mother feel better about moving away from Milwaukee, away from her sisters and other Indian relatives.

"There are Chippewas living all over northern Minnesota, Corrine."

My mother wants to know why we can't stop off at her Indian reservation, Odanah, to visit her cousin.

"Because we have to save on the gas," my father says. "We still got a long drive ahead. It'll be close to midnight before we get to Big Falls."

"Earl will borrow us some money," my mother replies.

"You don't even know if he's in Odanah."

"I just want to see Earl one last time."

"Where are all these papooses gonna sleep?"

"On the floor. Earl's got room."

"I said no. Now, damn it, Corrine, let's keep moving."

I sit up as much as I can until Dennis starts telling me to quit squirming around. I lean over my mother's shoulder and look into the snowflakes rushing straight at us, melting on the windshield.

Her black hair smells like perfume. I touch her warm, plump arms with the side of my face, and I close my eyes. I tap on Dennis's knee and whisper to him to tell me more. I want to tell him to speak up, that I can hear only some of what he says, but I know he can't.

I close my eyes, seeing my mother cooling in the snow, staring at that smoldering farmhouse grave.

She sits in my father's arms until the flames get smaller, until they turn to frozen ashes.

When my father rises, she does not take his hand. She will not go to the hospital to soothe the pain of those scorching snakes wrapped around her legs. She fears the touch of bandages, creams, and needles of white doctors more than the taste of fire venom.

So she suffers through the slow healing on her own with more snow, ice rags, and drugstore aspirin. She sits in silence with her memory, her father telling Chippewa stories during winter nights.

She remembers Odanah, the small town on the Bad River Indian Reservation along the frozen southern shores of Lake Superior. She remembers sitting with her sisters at the kitchen table. Her mother is in the next room at an old piano, practicing for Sunday Mass. My mother's father stuffs more wood in the barrel stove. He returns to the kitchen table to finish his story from long ago, a story about snakes with horns that rose to the surface of the Earth one day. But a storm of snow blew down from the stars. The Earth turned into ice, and the snakes were trapped above.

The piano music stops. My mother does not look up when she hears her mother's voice. "That's *not* how that story goes! You girls don't be listening. He's just making up his own crazy stories!"

But my mother keeps listening while swirling her fingertip on the wooden tabletop like an ink pen, practicing, wanting one day to write beautifully like the nuns at St. Mary's Indian School.

"The snakes waited until spring, when the Earth softened. They slipped out of their skins and slithered back into the melting ground," her father says. "Nanaboozhoo found those dry snake skins, crushed them into dust, and scattered them on the graves of those who had passed on."

The music stops again. My mother lifts her eyes above the table and looks into the living room. "That really true?" she asks her mother. "Graves covered with snake skins?"

Her mother closes her piano books and glares at her husband. "Stop telling those girls stories. They'll have nightmares about snakes all winter."

Her father laughs. "Well, she's right. That's all I got for now. I'll have to dream more about those snakes. Maybe I'll have more to tell tomorrow."

>[ ]<

The push of Dennis's knee against my back wakes me. The roar of my father's Oldsmobile cuts through the snow and night. I press my face against the window. The white-covered pine trees are getting taller and thicker the closer we get to Big Falls.

I close my eyes again and think about my mother's snake scars.

I can see her again. My mother is in the living room, surrounded by scorched walls and clear plastic taped over shattered windows. She is sitting next to a woodstove with a metal bucket. She dips a rag in her ice water and wraps it around her ankle.

While waiting for the burning in her legs to die down, she turns her fingertip into a pen and begins writing against the thin air.

My father closes the refrigerator door and pops open a can of beer. He turns to her, grinning. "What you writing, Corrine? Corrine?"

She pauses, then returns to her invisible letter, whispering out loud this time. "He never dreamed any more snake stories. Father died that night in his sleep. He doesn't have to dream about snakes anymore."

My mother suddenly pauses while reaching for another ice rag. She closes her eyes and lets out a long breath. Finally, in the last winter days of that fire year, the bite in her flesh removes its sting. But as she peels away layers of those healing rags, she sees that the snakes refuse to leave her. They do not return to the Earth. They cool and harden tight around my mother's calves and ankles.

>[ ]<

In the parking lot of a gas station in a place called Deer River, the night wind slaps against my face. But I don't feel it so much, following close to Dennis inside. Since we are the only ones still awake, my brother said he had some change in his pocket, maybe enough for a candy bar for us to split.

When we get back in the Oldsmobile, my father pulls out his watch, a watch that doesn't have a strap on it. "We have about an hour and a half of driving left," he says. "Should be there a little after midnight."

Once we reach the highway again, I lean my head against the backseat, making sure I can feel my mother's soft breathing again, making sure she is still asleep. And then I turn to Dennis, looking for his face in the darkness.

"When was I born?"

"Well, how old are you? Eight, right?"

"No, I mean, was I the first one born after that farm fire?"

I can hear him chewing the last of his half of the Charleston candy bar. He leans his face closer to mine and starts laughing. "How much you wanna bet the first place we stop off at once we get to Big Falls is a tavern?"

Darkness creeps up against the sides of the narrow highway. Suddenly moonlight peeks over the black wall of pine trees. I can see them more clearly now, pines pushing against each other, moving closer, surrounding us.

I turn away from the window.

I try thinking about things being different once we get to Big Falls—no more drinking, no more screaming, my mother making even bigger cinnamon rolls with her leftover bread dough.

But I can think only about Dennis and my dad and how they don't get along.

Dennis will turn fifteen this summer. He almost stayed behind, wanted to go live in a foster home like our two other brothers, James and Jerry. He thought about asking to stay with our oldest brother, Frankie. But Frankie lives in a one-room place downtown. So Dennis decided he should go with us. He didn't want Mom putting up with our dad's drinking and arguing all by herself.

I look out the window one more time, then quickly close my eyes, trying to keep the trees from coming closer.

"What are you scared of?" Dennis says to me. "There's nothing out there, nothing except sticks." And then he says it again, only louder this time for our father to hear. "Nothing up here except sticks!"

I squeeze my eyes tighter and get as close to the floor of the Oldsmobile as I can. I try to think about my mother baking her bread. I try to imagine sitting around the kitchen table with Dennis listening to our mother talk about her Indian sisters, how they like to drink and laugh, call up their cousin Earl in the middle of the night and ask him to settle a fight about the correct way to say certain Indian words. But suddenly in my mind, my mother is alone. She is alone with her bread dough in that farmhouse kitchen. She is thinner. Her green dress is brighter, not yet stained with grease. My father staggers into the house. When he takes off his cap to rub his head, the gray hair is gone. It's turned back to brown. He makes a crooked smile at my mother as he digs for a pack of crumpled cigarettes in his coat pocket.

When she sees his smile, she stops pushing her fists into the bread dough. She stops scrubbing the wood floors, stops feeding clothes through the washing machine wringer. She screams at my father. Why did he have to spend the last of the food money? Why did he stop off at the tavern? How could he even think of drinking when they've got all these kids to feed? Why would he spend what little they had when she doesn't have one damn decent pair of nylon stockings? Suddenly the only thing I can see are my mother's snake scars.

"Hey! Wake up. You're talking in your sleep."

I open my eyes and feel Dennis's hand on my shoulder. "We're almost there."

"What happened next?" I ask.

"Wake up. You're dreaming."

"After the fire, Dennis? What happened next?"

My brother laughs, then whispers. "What do you think happened? The fire trucks left and Dad went to the tavern."

"What about Mom?"

Dennis is silent.

"Just tell me. Tell me about Mom."

My mother stays on that farm for as long as she can. Her anger settles down into silence. She sits for hours in that kitchen holding the broom. She wants the Earth to open up again.

Some nights when my father comes in after working in the barn, he finds the gas oven left on. When he has to take over washing the diapers, his work overhauls, and the rest of the clothes, he finds books of matches in her dress pockets. In the mornings, before heading out to milk the cows, he watches her from the kitchen doorway. He asks what she plans to do for the day. She just sits there, tapping the end of the broomstick on the linoleum floor.

Finally my father drives to town to find a pay phone to make a call.

"She went to the hospital to get help?" I ask.

"Just listen," Dennis says.

At night the nurse takes my mother's dinner tray, shuts out the light, and locks the door from the other side.

My mother moves to the window and looks past the white metal bars. She stares into the white moon. She stares into the shadows of naked oak trees covering the frozen Earth, listening for a faraway train. She presses her cheek against the cold bars. She lifts her finger to the glass and begins to write a letter.

"Who did she write to?"

"I don't know. Maybe Aunt Sylvia."

. . . It looks like they'll let me go next week. Don will pick up the papooses from the foster home this weekend. He says he found a cheap three-bedroom duplex in Milwaukee to rent. He's going back to working construction again.

They have no television in this place, and I've read every magazine I could get my hands on. I got another one due in December. I'm sure it's a boy again. I don't know what I'll name this one. I'm running out of names.

It'll be good to get back to the city. I can't remember the last time I seen a show. Maybe we could see that new Elizabeth Taylor movie that's coming out. Or, at the very least, maybe I can talk Don into buying a used television set. I'll need something to pass the time. The doctor says I need to take it slow. But after this one is born, I don't know what I'll do. Don won't quit drinking. He'll get sick of the city and want to go back to farming again. So, no, I don't know what I'll do if we leave again.

>[ ]<

The moon begins to slip away just as my father's Oldsmobile pulls up to a stop sign. Deserted streets. Big Falls.

We're all awake now—Dennis, Joseph, John, my sister Philly, and my younger brothers, Scott, Michael, and the baby, Robert. We fight for a view of the barely lit town covered in snow. Dennis points out that there are two taverns, Hagen's Corner Bar and Municipal Liquors. My father slows his Oldsmobile. But the lights in the taverns are already going out. The parking lots are filled with headlights and clouds of exhaust.

My father tells us he'll have to spend money on a motel tonight— money he "really doesn't have"—but with all the new snow, the Oldsmobile would never make it up the farm driveway.

In the motel room, my mother sits on the edge of the bed, peeling down her new pair of nylon stockings that she bought at Ben

Franklin before we moved away from Milwaukee. She doesn't know that I am watching her as she slowly touches the snake scars wrapped around her legs.

My father turns out the light. My mother looks up into the moon falling down on her face. My father reaches for the curtains, but she whispers, "No, Don. Let the moon be."

My father and Michael take one bed, and my mother sleeps in the other one with Robert and Philly. The rest of us find spots on the carpeted floor, sharing pillows.

I drift away for the last time tonight. I think about seeing my mother touching those snake scars. Since the day I was born, those scars have never moved. I wonder if they will ever disappear, if one day my mother will have smooth legs again, if she can go into town without having to wear those nylon stockings, if one day my mother can go into the store and buy her hairspray, her eyebrow pencil, and a new dress without worrying if people are talking about her.

One day, one year soon, when the Earth is freed from the iron snows of winter, those snakes will crawl out of my mother's burned skin, giving up their grip on her. They will slither back into the hot mud of the Earth. This time the snakes will expect her to follow. And she will.

⟩[2]⟨

An Ancient Winter

My father says this is the year of an ancient winter. Winters can live to be a thousand years old in northern Minnesota. Fleeing the warm winds of spring, a winter can hide in the tops of thick pines, under the heaviness of bogs turned to stone, and along the still shores of sleeping lakes and slow rivers. A winter can grow old without tiring this far north. It still has the muscle to shatter the clouds into a thousand snows. It can return the Earth back into ice as it spreads its wings across blue skies, keeping the sun cold, diminishing the days.

I get my first daylight view of the oldness of winter at our new farm a mile away from Big Falls. I wipe away the frost from the Oldsmobile window and stare across white fields that look like an ocean, rolling white waves frozen in time.

We are parked on the side of a dirt road, waiting for a county snowplow to open up the driveway that leads to the new farmhouse.

My brothers, Philly, and I quietly eat the last of the cold egg sandwiches and pass around a plastic gallon of fruit punch. Our dog, Whiskey, snatches the rest of my sandwich from my hand as I try to see the end of those fields of snow that have not been touched in years.

My father says we are forty miles south of the Canadian border as he turns the radio dial. We hear only screeching static.

"Oh, turn that damn noise off," my mother says as she wipes the steamy frost from her window to get a clearer view of the nothingness. "Why now? Why couldn't you wait until June or even April?"

My father grins as he takes in the last breath of smoke from his rolled cigarette. "They say it can snow even in June up in these parts."

A radio announcer breaks into the static. He says something about the first day of spring waking up like a lion and something about Koochiching County getting hit the worst, close to a foot of snow in Big Falls alone.

When the snowplow finally arrives, when it slams the last of the snow into another mountain, my father steers his Oldsmobile down the white driveway, parking it next to a garage, not the farmhouse. My mother clings to Robert and refuses to get out of the car. My father lets the engine stay running but reaches to turn off the radio. My mother tells him to leave it on.

My father orders my older brothers to start unloading the U-Haul trailer while he finds wood for the barrel stove in the garage. That's where we'll sleep tonight. It's where the previous family lived after the farmhouse caught fire.

"There was a fire here, too?" Dennis asks as he buttons up his brown corduroy coat. "Look at that old house. It's ready to collapse."

I finish buckling my black rubber boots. I have to give my mittens to John to wear for unloading the trailer. I am the first one to escape from the Oldsmobile. Philly follows me. Together we fight against the winter by trudging through snowdrifts that reach up to our waists. Whiskey, who is not even a year old yet, steps in our tracks. His fur is as almost as white as the snow. Only a patch of brown on his chest keeps him from being swallowed whole by the drifts.

We finally make our way to the new house, a falling-down building with a crushed-in cement porch and black smoke scars that rise up along two stories of cracked cement. My father yells, forbids my sister and me from going into the house. Philly grabs me by the shoulder and tells me to wait. When our father disappears into the garage with an armful of chopped wood, Whiskey and I follow her inside.

The winter owns the five-bedroom farmhouse. Snow mounds cover the hardwood floors. The wind comes and goes as it pleases through broken windows. There is not much left of the family who moved out of here after the fire—a few scattered tennis shoes, a ripped gray couch that has no legs or cushions. Philly finds a small, light-blue suitcase. She wonders if anyone will come back for it. I tell her to keep it, but she shakes her head no, then snaps it shut. She grabs my shoulder again and tells me she wants to see the rest of the house.

The basement is a skating rink; a foot of thick, clear ice stretches wall to wall. The cold sunlight streams down on the ice through the dusty windows. Whiskey barks at us as we run and slide across the ice. When our bare hands turn pink, my sister says she needs to go back to the car to warm up.

Whiskey and I stay, sitting on the ice. The building is as silent as a graveyard. The cracked cement walls are like a castle, as ancient as the ocean of snow that surrounds the farm. I remember the night my father came back to our duplex apartment on the south side of Milwaukee. He rode the Greyhound bus to Big Falls to sign the farm papers. He was gone almost a week. The first question my mother asked him was if the land was worth farming, and if it was, then why did that family sell so cheap?

"People were never raised to be farmers around Big Falls because most of the land is swamp," he told her. "They mine the trees up there—loggers who race to work the frozen forests before it thaws. But I bought eighty acres, forty of it cleared, dry enough to plant hay, maybe even oats if I want. Hell, I can make a go of it with forty acres any day. I was raised a farmer."

Suddenly Whiskey claws at the ice, trying to dig up a dead squirrel stuck below the surface. Its eyes are wide open, its claws showing. A blast of wind screams through the farmhouse. It's time to get back to my father's Oldsmobile.

There is a gray barn and a chicken coop behind the garage. A row of pine trees runs along the front yard between the farm and dirt road. The only survivors of this long winter are four crows standing on an electric pole. Whiskey barks at them, and they squawk back. He barks again, but they refuse to leave. Before I follow the tracks back to my mother, I notice smoke coming out of the garage chimney, rising, disappearing in the blue sky. My father is standing in the cleared driveway with his rolled cigarette. He is not wearing his winter coat, just his cap and heavy underwear shirt with long sleeves. His hands are on his hips. He is turning slowly, trying to catch the full view of his farmland. But I know he can't see as much as he wants. The waves of snow go on forever across the fields.

>[ ]<

It will take the spring and part of the summer before we can move into the farmhouse. My father says the southern wall is caving in, that he and the older boys will have to set up some wood poles to keep it steady.

Philly and John take turns washing and drying the dinner dishes. My mother shoves her cardboard boxes of pots and pans under the sink because there are no shelves in this garage. She orders Joseph to empty the slop bucket out back. The people before us built a small bathroom and put in a toilet. But my father says we can't use it. The pipes are frozen. My mother says nothing else as she watches my father sitting at the kitchen table with his construction pencil and a glass of buttermilk, figuring out other costs such as enough cement to "reinforce the farmhouse foundation."

When he goes out to chop more wood for the stove, my mother tells Dennis she is just waiting for that day to come when our father starts drinking again.

Dennis says he knows how it will happen, just like always.

She will go into town with him to get the mail at the post office and some hamburger, tomato sauce, flour, and yeast at the Red Owl grocery store. She will dress up as much as she can—hairspray, red lipstick, and eyebrow pencil. She will put on her long, black wool coat, the one she bought at the Salvation Army for the move to Big Falls. He will drop her off to do her shopping, and he'll say he's going to get some gas at the station a half mile away off Highway 71. Inside the Red Owl, she will only smile at the lady standing behind the meat counter wrapping hamburger in a sheet of white waxed paper. At the counter, she will politely ask the cashier to put it all in just one bag.

"How come only one bag?" I ask.

"Because when she comes out of the Red Owl and sees the Oldsmobile parked in front of Hagen's Corner Bar, one bag is all she'll be able to carry when she walks the mile home," Dennis says.

Suddenly the front door swings open. Our father is carrying firewood. "I'm thinking we should get some chickens when it warms up," he says. "Some good layers."

Dennis gets up from the table and asks if he can take the radio into the bedroom. He promises to put it back on top of the refrigerator before going to bed.

My mother tells me to feed Whiskey the mashed potato leftovers. I take the pot off the stove and place it on the cement floor. I sit next to Whiskey and stroke his back.

"I've been going over that chicken coop," my father says. "It's insulated, but I'm still gonna buy an incubator."

When Whiskey finishes, I put on Dennis's corduroy coat, and we head outside into the cold dusk air.

More spring snow is falling. Whiskey and I walk up to the dirt road and stand, staring toward the highway. Two monster logging trucks rumble along Highway 71. We listen for the distant train that comes by this time of the day. A rabbit hops across the road. Whiskey takes off and chases after it into the ditch, sinking in snow until finally he has to turn back. The rabbit disappears into a thick forest of barren willow bushes. I dust the snow from the dog's head and look to the highway again. Our first day of school in Big Falls is tomorrow. The bus will turn off Highway 71 and come down the long dirt road. Whiskey will be the first one out the door. But once my brothers, sister, and I run and reach the top of the driveway, I'll grab Whiskey to keep him from getting on the bus with us. I'll hold him tight and look back at the garage for as long as I can until the driver says we can't wait any longer.

❖[3]❖

Cloud Ceremony

On the day before Easter Sunday, the clouds finally thaw, turning from snow to rain. Warm winds return as the winter weakens, drips away from the skies. The trees along the dirt road and beyond begin to move again, shaking off the melting ice from their pine-needle skins.

I see a flash of lightning streak across the grayness, then a crash of thunder bangs on the clouds like a drum. I can hear my younger brother Scott yelling at me to "get inside!" I look away from the skies and see Michael trying to keep up with Scott, holding up his baggy pants, both splashing through loose snow and mud and slipping their way to the barn. We've been out here all afternoon exploring, finding buried winter treasures that the snows hid—a rusty tricycle, a baseball glove, and a G.I. Joe doll with one leg missing.

Inside the barn, I listen to the rain rattling on the roof while my brothers try twisting a twig into G.I. Joe's hip, wanting to give him a new leg.

The barn is empty now, but my father plans on buying some cows once his next veterans check comes in the mail. He says we'll save a lot of money on milk and finally have real butter. And he says fresh milk tastes better than store milk. But even if it doesn't,

we just know it has to taste better than what we do drink—
powdered milk.

We wait until the rain slows down, then make a dash for the
garage. Whiskey spots us from the broken cement porch of the
farmhouse and races toward us. The house is lit from a long extension cord running from the garage. My father and older brothers
put up the beams a week ago to keep the house from falling in.
This weekend they have been scraping old, hard pig and chicken
crap from two of the bedrooms. My father says he has no idea why
that family turned the farmhouse into a barn after the fire.

As soon as we get inside the garage, Scott and I stand next to
the woodstove and hang our wet heads over it to dry. We giggle
when the drops of rain hit the stove, turn to steam, and rise back
up into our faces. Scott whispers that maybe we won't have to take
a bath for church tomorrow. Whiskey shakes the rain from his fur,
and I do the same. My mother yells at me to "cut that shit out!"

After I finish drying my hair, I hand the towel to Scott. I stand in
the bathroom doorway, looking at my mother and Philly in the
kitchen. My sister reads from her catechism book while my mother
hangs round slices of pineapple on her ham. My mother has been
preparing Easter dinner all day. Her bread dough is puffing up over
the edges of the pans. The potatoes have already been peeled, sliced,
and placed in a kettle of water. In the early morning, she will start
the ham in the oven. Once we get home from church, she will have
the potatoes boiled and mashed. The corn will be steaming, her
bread cooled and sliced.

We've been to St. Joseph's every Sunday since moving to Big
Falls, but my mother has always stayed home. Every week she tells
my father that she does not have a decent dress to wear and that her
only pair of nylons has too many holes in them.

"What the hell you worried about a dress for?" my father always says. "No one's gonna be staring at you. It's church, for Christ's sake."

I sit next to my sister and her catechism book and pretend to be reading with her. But I am really just trying to get a closer look at my mother's green dress covered in flour and grease stains.

>[ ]<

The only television channel we get comes from a big city in Canada, Winnipeg. My mother was hoping there would be that movie about the Ten Commandments, but the only show on television is a hockey game. My mother tells us to shut it off.

In the kitchen, my father pounds off the lid of his milk can with a hammer. He keeps his papers and old photographs in that can, keeps them safe from us kids and just in case there's a house fire. My mother clears a spot on the small counter next to the sink and begins to roll out her bread dough.

My father takes off his thick glasses and rubs his eyes. He says the first farm payment is due in May, not June like he thought.

"Damn, I was planning on getting four Holsteins next month," he tells my mother.

"Did you already order those chickens?"

"That's another thing. I still have to buy an incubator."

"How much is that gonna cost us?" my mother asks.

"What the hell does that mean? It's gonna cost whatever it costs. I'm trying to get this farm going!"

There is really no place to go when my father starts in about money and other things that he likes to argue about. The garage has only two bedrooms. The thin walls cannot keep out the anger.

"How much is it gonna cost?" my father yells. "What kind of a damn question is that?"

"It's a damn good question," my mother says. "Because besides your chickens, you got a bar tab to pay—Hagen's? How much is that gonna cost?"

Turning up the radio as far as it will go won't drown out the yelling.

"No one's starving around here. What about that ham? You think I got that for free?"

Going outside would help, but I can't because the liners of my boots are soaked.

"Just one damn half-decent dress," my mother says. "That's all I asked for."

"I don't know how many times I told you! There's a Salvation Army store right downtown in International Falls the size of Penney's!"

So I sit there in that big garage until that anger is done yelling at me.

"I don't have a thing to wear!"

"It's just church, for Christ's sake!"

"To hell with it, Don! I am not going!"

Finally my mother slams her bread pan on the counter and reaches for the broom. She sits in front of the television, staring into the black screen, tapping the tip of the broom on the floor. Whiskey quickly moves to her and sits at her feet. My father storms over to the television, turns it on, then rips the broom from her hand.

"If you're gonna watch TV, then watch it!" he says. "For Christ's sake, Corrine. I'm not gonna go through this shit again!"

My mother says nothing.

He stares at her for a minute, then moves back to his milk can.

>[ ]<

I sit frozen at the other end of the table. I watch my father sort through birth certificates, his Oldsmobile papers, and black and white photographs. I wait until he bends down to dig out more milk can papers, and then I sneak one of the photographs under my shirt. It's a picture of my mother and father when they were young, when my mother was skinny.

I take the photograph to the bedroom. Dennis and John are playing rummy. Joseph is reading his Thor and Captain America comic books. I sit on the mattress on the floor next to Dennis and show him the photograph. He only glances at it and draws a card from the deck.

"Think the Easter Bunny will show up this year?" John asks, grinning behind the cards he's holding.

"Oh, yeah! He'll be here, alright," Dennis says, sounding like our father, making fun of him. "Chocolate eggs, marshmallow rabbits, and all the jelly beans you kids can eat!"

They burst into laughter, but I just stare at the photograph. The only time I remember having any Easter candy was when Robert was born. He was so sick he almost died. My mother stayed in the hospital with him. When the social worker came by to check on my sister and younger brothers, she brought us each a small construction paper basket filled with jelly beans and glittery grass.

Dennis throws his cards down and reaches in his shirt pocket. He takes out a handful of my dad's tobacco and some papers. He tells Joseph to give him one of his comic books.

"Show me that photograph again," he says to me while rolling cigarettes on the comic book. "You steal that from the old man's milk can?"

Lately Dennis has been calling our father "the old man." He told our mother that the older he gets, the more he realizes what a no-good drunk the old man is and that he can't bring himself to call a drunk his dad.

Dennis stares at the black and white photograph. Our mother is wearing a new dress, maybe red or blue but probably the same green dress she always wears. Our father is dressed in a suit coat and tie. They are sitting together around a table with her sisters and his white relatives. Dennis hands the photograph back to me and says the old man had to quit school in the eighth grade and become the man of the family.

"Why?" I ask.

"Because his dad died suddenly," Dennis says. "Had a heart attack while out plowing."

Even though my father had to take over the farm, he and his mother never talked much. His youngest brother and sister died of scarlet fever. His mother hated him for that, said he carried the disease home one day from school.

"But then the old man got his chance to get away from her. He joined the war," Dennis says. "He was sent to Fort Snelling in Minneapolis. That's where he learned to drink. That's where he was stationed the day Pearl Harbor was bombed by the Japanese. The old man met Mom when he returned from Germany. He bought Mom and her sisters drinks one night at a bar in Milwaukee. They were married in a Catholic church. After the ceremony, they drank until the next morning at a VFW hall somewhere on the south side. That's where the photograph came from."

Suddenly I hear my father slamming his milk can shut with the hammer.

"You better hide that photo under the bed," Dennis says. "I'll put it back in that milk can when the old man's not looking."

Dennis slips three rolled cigarettes into his shirt pocket and nods at John and Joseph. Before they leave, John turns off the light. I hear the front door open, then my father asking where the three of them are going. Dennis tells him they're going for a walk down the dirt road. I hear the front door close.

I can never sleep with the TV blaring, so I pull some bits of cotton from a hole in the mattress and stuff them in my ears. I wait until the room gets brighter from the light coming in under the door, then I stare at my mother in that photograph for as long as I can keep my eyes open.

Ever since we moved to Big Falls, Dennis sometimes shows up in my dreams. Usually he's got his school backpack stuffed with his clothes. He's always leaving—walking down the dirt road to the highway, sticking his thumb out, waiting for one of those logging trucks to give him a ride to Minneapolis, then another truck ride to Milwaukee.

Dennis likes telling me about our mother wanting to leave the Indian reservation when she was younger. She couldn't wait to move to Milwaukee to be with her older sisters, Sylvia, Philomena, and Victoria.

And in my dreams, he likes telling me things about my mother that even he does not know.

Look closer at Mom in that photograph. She is really not looking into the camera, is she? If you stare deeper into her eyes, you will see she is really looking up. She's looking for the clouds. Now follow her eyes. See? She is drifting above the glasses of beer, slices of white cake, and lunchmeat sandwiches, higher than the fireworks of laughter and the champagne balloons hanging from the ceiling.

Notice the look on Mom's sisters and her new husband's booze buddies. None of them can see her floating away. Look how they raise their glasses high for the camera. But once they hear that click, once they almost blink at the bright flashing of the bulb, Mom is already long gone, isn't she?

Look up. See? She rises between the rafters, through the tar shingles, above the city sky—turning the black and white wedding into color, landing on some heavy orange cloud, sitting against a blue sky. Mom is looking down on her future.

She sees there will be more laughter spilling over the tops of beer glasses. There will be more drinking, the kind that lasts longer than the happiness—the kind that turns into rage. She will count the bruises (not too many). She will count the leftover quarters and dimes found in the pockets of her husband as he sleeps off a night of drinking away the rent and grocery money. There will be a new child almost every year. There will be the separate beds, the end of touching. They will share a signature or two to find a bigger duplex to rent, another burnt-out farm, a used car. When a basement beam breaks her husband's construction back, it'll be months before his veterans disability kicks in. They will have to sign together when applying for county assistance that will feed all those faces sitting around the table—and pay for more of his drinking. But there will be no shared signing of saying good-bye. She will wish it, but where would she go with all these papooses? Where?

So for now, during this moment in the autumn of 1956, Corrine Winifred Bennett Rolo will decide to leave the clouds and float back down inside the VFW hall and sit at her new husband's side. She will look back up one more time at the colors of the sky, then turn to her new husband and answer, yes, yes, she would be very honored to pour him, Donald James Rolo, another glass of beer.

>[ ]<

On the morning of our first Easter in Big Falls, Minnesota, I open my eyes to sunlight pouring through clouds and through the bedroom window. My brothers are still sleeping, so I am careful in stepping over their bodies to get to the door.

In the kitchen I see my mother standing behind a chair, brushing my sister's hair. She tells Philly to "recite it again."

My sister turns back a page in her catechism book. "I believe in God, the Father almighty, creator of heaven and earth . . ."

And then my mother brushes her own hair. She tells Philly to get her little mirror and lipstick in her black purse. My mother sets down the brush and reaches for the dishrag. She rinses it under the cold water faucet. My mother stands in the window light with that rag and washes away, as best she can, the flour and grease from her green dress.

›[4]‹

A Howling Loon

My mother never goes out at night.

She never strolls across the wet fields to stand in the face of the late spring moon, never steps into the brown forest to stare into the eyes of the watching owl. My mother fears the creatures that have awakened from their winter graves, those that once again roam the night woods.

"Black bears don't eat people," my father tells her while sitting with his legs crossed at the kitchen table, holding his cup of buttermilk.

"My mother used to have nightmares about bears after my father died," my mother softly says as she locks the front door. "The dreams got so bad she didn't dare fall asleep, all alone in that bed, alone out there in the sticks." And then she shakes her head and mumbles, "Stuck out in the sticks and not a damn thing she could do about it."

I finish wiping down the counter and look at my father. His head is down now, staring at the cement floor. My mother reaches for her blue sweater hanging on a nail next to the woodstove. She bought that blue sweater in town this morning. A fat white lady who was having a rummage sale wanted to give it to my mother for free when she realized the zipper was broken. But my mother wanted to pay the quarter for it instead. I move out of her way when she reaches for the drawer underneath the countertop. She digs out her round Christmas cookie can filled with her needles and spools of thread. My father is still staring at the floor. Finally he takes the last drink of his buttermilk. My mother sits down across from him at the table.

"How long before we can move into the farmhouse?" she asks my father.

"Soon as I can afford to buy a new picture window for the dining room. Next month," he says. "Hard to say. The transmission in the Oldsmobile is going out."

She wets the end of her thread, then feeds it through a needle. He stares at her.

"Maybe August you can go back to visit, before school starts again," my father says. "Maybe I can save up enough for a bus ticket."

"What about those chickens?"

"Yes, the hens should start laying by then. You can put up a sign in the Laundromat."

"We don't have a phone."

"Tell 'em to come out to the Rolo place. Everyone knows who we are now." He stands with his cup and goes to the sink. "Corrine, it's the best I can do. We're on a fixed income here."

My mother sets her sweater in her lap. "I'm almost out of writing paper," she says.

"Yes, I know," my father says.

"I want some new pens. Those kids keep taking mine. When you get your check tomorrow . . ."

"Yes, you can pick out whatever you need from the hardware store."

"You pick it up. I'm not going into town. The baby's sick."

"Just tell me what you need."

"A book of stamps, too. I got envelopes but no stamps."

>[ ]<

After school, Scott and I decide to skip catching the bus ride home. We stay on the playground with the kids who live in town, playing softball until too many of them have to go home for supper. Scott waves good-bye with his glove, and we head uptown to Hagen's Corner Bar. We know our father will be there.

The bar is nearly full with sawmill workers who come in at the end of the day. Our father sits alone on the far end of the bar, smoking a filter cigarette. He always buys real cigarettes when he drinks. When he sees us, he slaps the stool next to him and tells us to order ourselves some Cokes and potato chips. "You boys gotta eat, right?"

There is a brown Hardware Hank paper bag sitting on the bar next to my dad's beer bottle. I can see the edge of a notebook sticking out of the bag.

The bar owner, Red, rubs the back of his buzz-cut hair and fills two glasses of ice with soda. Scott doesn't like to talk around other people because he stutters most of the time, so I order the Old Dutch potato chips.

"Listen, you boys," my father says after sipping from his bottle of beer. "Those chicks I ordered last month will be coming tomorrow—a hundred and fifty of 'em. I'm gonna be counting on you boys to make sure that incubator doesn't go out. They all ain't gonna make it. Not all of them do, maybe a hundred, maybe more. Can't depend on your mother. She's got too much worrying on her mind these days. So I'm counting on you boys to do your best to keep those chicks warm."

"What is Mom worrying about?" Scott asks.

I quickly shove my hand against my brother's shoulder and tell him to stop talking.

"You just leave the worrying to me," our father says. "You boys just make sure you keep those chicks alive."

Scott and I finish our Cokes and lick our fingers. Our father is now going on about serving in World War II, dodging bombs and bullets in Germany. We know enough to keep nodding when he starts in on the war. But we also know he can go on forever. Finally, once he slips off his stool and staggers to the bathroom, I grab that brown paper bag with the writing paper in it and push my brother toward the door.

Just as we get about a half mile out of town, we see Joseph coming down the highway. We know it's him because we can hear his leather boots clicking on the tarred road. It's also light enough to get a good look at his wide-open eyes glaring at us even before he gets close. My first thought is that he found out Scott and I have been reading his new comic books. He tries to hide them underneath his stack of old ones.

Joseph reaches out and grabs the paper bag from my hand and opens it. He asks if the Bic pens and stamps are in the bag as well. "Mom's been waiting for this stuff," he says. He points his finger at us and tells us, "Get moving!"

"Hey, Joseph!" I say. "We saved you a trip into town!"

"Yeah, you did. But Mom's pretty pissed at you guys for missing the bus. Now, get moving!"

As our older brother marches us ahead of him, I pull my arms out of my shirtsleeves, folding them against my bare chest to keep warm. The farther away from Big Falls we get, the growing stillness of the woods and the clicking of Joseph's boots echoing through the trees make me wish we were closer than we are to home.

I think even Joseph is afraid. He tries to break the cold silence by bringing up the latest Captain America comic. "Spider-Man guest-stars," he says. "Do you wanna know what happens?"

"No. I wanna know why we can't live in town like everyone else."

"What?" Joseph says.

"Why can't the old man work at the sawmill like everybody else's dad? Why do we have to live in a stupid garage on a stupid burnt-out farm?" And then I turn to the woods and scream even louder. "Why do we have to live out here in the sticks?"

I feel Joseph's hand on my shoulders, turning me around to face him. "Do you wanna hear about Captain America and Spider-Man or not?"

"We already read it," Scott says.

"What?"

I look across the wet ditch into the forest of pines. They just stare back at us, listening to our every word. I push my arms back into my shirtsleeves, then reach down to pick up a handful of stones. I whip those stones as far as I can at those trees. I throw more stones, again and again until I can't feel the cold anymore. I almost grab more stones, but I know it won't make a difference. Those trees won't stop. They'll just keep standing there, watching us.

I feel Joseph's hand on my shoulder again, turning me back to the highway. I march like he wants me to. But this time, he doesn't let go. This time, he walks beside me.

>[ ]<

My mother usually lets us soak the pots and pans when we do dishes, but not tonight. Scott and I do not dare fight over who gets to use the good metal scrubber while she sits at the kitchen table with her broom. My mother figured out a long time ago, probably before I was born, that when it came to getting after us for not listening or not doing what we were told, the reach of the broom worked better than trying to chase after us.

Even with the television volume turned down, my mother isn't getting very much letter writing done with all of us in the garage. She chews the end of her Bic pen under a dirty yellow light bulb. Whiskey sleeps on the cement floor at her feet. He follows my mother around more than any of us now that we're in school all week. A few times, when my father couldn't get the Oldsmobile started, Whiskey walked to town with her to mail letters to her sisters.

I show the last rinsed pan to my mother. She nods, and I put it in the dish tray. I steal a quick drink from the faucet. My mother doesn't like it when we drink without a cup even though I never touch the faucet with my lips. She gets up from the table, rips her letter, then tosses it in the woodbin by the stove. She puts her pen in her dress pocket and moves to the front door. She tells all of us that we'd better get some sleep soon because "when your father comes home drunk, you know he's gonna start raising Cain."

I watch my mother reach for the flashlight on top of the refrigerator, then call Whiskey. I sneak to the front door and open it enough to see her standing in the driveway. She watches the dog under a streak of red sunlight and a dark blue sky. Philly quickly puts down her math book and gets up from the couch. She races to the woodbin and takes out some of the ripped pieces of the letter, putting them together. I tell her to read it out loud while I stand by the door.

... There's not a thing to do up here. The closest Penney's is forty miles away. I can't watch my shows. We only get one channel up here. Just about every program is in French ... I should never have let Don talk me into leaving. All I do is bake bread and do laundry ... her name is Irene Cloutier. She's French, I guess. She had a rummage sale in town. I was hoping to find a dress, and when I met Irene, I thought I might. Irene is

*as big as I am. We had coffee and cookies at her sale . . . said we should
have coffee sometime, and she wrote down her number. I told her I would
call even though we don't have a phone . . . by the end of July I can start
selling some eggs . . . I'd like to have a decent dress when I take the Greyhound to visit. We can't even afford layaway at Penney's, but I have my
eye on a nice pink rayon dress with purple violet flowers . . .*

I hear my mother calling me to bring her blue sweater hanging on
the wall. I grab it and head outside without my shoes or socks on.
The gravel stones feel like ice cubes, so I take bigger steps.

She zips up her sweater and calls the dog.

"Where are you going, Mom?"

"Nowhere," she says as she scratches behind Whiskey's ears. "I'm
just going to take a look inside the house."

I don't follow her as she and Whiskey walk toward the farmhouse. My mother likes to be alone even when she's with us, even
when she's laughing while telling stories to my brother Dennis. If
she knew I was following her, I'd end up scrubbing dishes all by
myself tomorrow night and probably the next night, too.

My mother has never been in the farmhouse. She told my father
she didn't trust those broken cement porch steps. He replaced a
couple of rotted wood steps on the back porch and said she should
go inside and look over the kitchen, that she'd like the size of it
and that he was going to build her brand-new cupboards and a big
countertop for rolling out her bread dough.

I wait until she gets close to the back porch. Then I circle around
through the frosty grass, standing behind one of the willow trees as
high as the farmhouse. I watch as my mother looks over those new
steps. She doesn't trust that porch, either. She flashes her light
inside the busted kitchen window. I wish I had the guts to go up to
my mother and tell her that I would climb up those back steps with

her flashlight, that I would find the extension cord and plug it in so the kitchen lights would come on. But I think I'm more afraid of the dark than anyone in the family.

My feet can't take the cold anymore, so I sit down next to the willow tree. I blow on my hands and rub my toes. The red sun has almost disappeared. My mother clicks off her flashlight. I think of making a fast break for the garage. But she does not call the dog and head back. Instead she crosses the yard to the edge of the fields. She watches a bird splashing its wings in one of the field ponds left behind by winter. She listens as the bird screams, makes a howling sound. I wait for Whiskey to go chasing after that bird, but he doesn't move. He just sits next to my mother and watches, listens with her.

I have never seen a real loon before. And I don't know if I have ever heard their calling out to each other. My brother John brings home a lot of books from the school library. Our father once asked him to look up all the different kinds of animals that live in "these parts." John showed us pictures of the loon. He read about how they fly south during the wintertime, as far away as San Diego, California. He read about how the loon always returns to northern places like Minnesota and Wisconsin. John read about their calling sound, how they have an "eerie, lonely, beautiful cry." But sometimes the loon will howl. I asked John what the book said about a howling loon. He just shrugged and said he didn't know. "Maybe the loon howls when she is all alone."

The loon lifts her head from the icy pond. She howls again, then flaps her wings, startled when she realizes we are watching. She rises above the field and into the darkest part of the blue sky. I can no longer see her. And when I look back to the Earth, my mother is gone, too.

⟩[5]⟨

Feast of Memory

Lately my mother has been watching more television without the set turned on. I catch her staring at herself in the mirror of the screen of our turned-off Zenith black-and-white set. Once I crawled along the cement floor, reached my hand up, and switched it on. I made my getaway while it took a minute for the TV to warm up. I tried sitting behind my brothers at the kitchen table, but she picked me out with her eyes and said maybe it was time to get the broom.

When we get back from church, my father goes straight to the chicken coop to check on the chicks. I see my mother sitting in front of the blank television screen.

This morning was the first time Dennis decided he was not going to church anymore. My father told him that he had two choices: "Either go with the rest of us or pack your clothes and hitchhike back to Milwaukee." Dennis just pulled the covers over his head.

He is still sleeping when I open the bedroom door. I tell him he has to get up because our mother is watching television again. I tell him the old man is going to be coming back from the chicken coop any minute. He jumps up and I get out of his way.

Dennis is the only one who can get our mother to snap out of watching TV. He teases her about dyeing her hair, trying to be like a white woman. He brings up stories about her sisters—like "getting bombed on New Year's Eve" and "falling on their asses in the snow." Our mother starts laughing so hard she gets tears in her eyes.

When he's not around, we sometimes try other things like knocking on the front door or pulling out the mattresses into the living room and playing football. Sometimes Scott and I sit in front of the TV and make faces at our mother's reflection on the blank screen.

But the one thing my brothers, sister, and I never do is tell our mother the house is on fire.

When Dennis sees our mother on the couch holding Robert, he yells at John to get to the front door and watch for the old man. He kneels in front of our mother and touches her shoulder. "Mom? The old man's gonna start shit with me about skipping church. Mom? I don't wanna fight with him. Mom?"

She doesn't blink her eyes.

"Mom? You need to get up. Come on. I'll peel the potatoes."

I stand in front of the television, but she still stares.

"Mom? If you don't get up, the old man's gonna drive into town and call the hospital in Littlefork. Did you hear me, Mom? He's gonna call the damn hospital on you!"

Finally Robert starts crying in our mother's arms. She slowly looks down at him, opens her dress, and pulls him to her bare breast. We wait until she finally looks at Dennis. She whispers when she tells him to check the roast, that he needs to turn the stove on high for the potatoes.

Dennis lets out a big breath and looks at me. "Turn on the TV," he says. "See if there's something worth watching besides a damn church show."

I know one day Dennis is going to pack his clothes and leave, probably when he turns fifteen this summer. He doesn't like going to high school in Littlefork. That's where he and Joseph have to go since Big Falls has school only through sixth grade. Littlefork is a twenty-mile bus ride each way. Dennis says most of his teachers don't like him because he's Indian. He has one teacher who calls him *Chief* and another one who says he should just drop out and move back to the reservation and live off the government.

Dennis wanted to join the track team this spring, but our father said there was no way he could afford to drive that many miles to pick him up after practice. But even if our father could afford that, he wouldn't. Every night, including weekends, Dennis, Joseph, and John have to work with him on fixing up the farmhouse.

One night when we got off the school bus, Dennis walked right in the garage and told the old man that he could not paint, scrub, or sand any more hardwood floors because he had a big test to study for. "There is no way in hell I'm going to drop out of high school and spend the rest of my life on this damn farm."

He argued back and forth with the old man until the fistfighting started. Dennis ended up running to the barn and hiding in the hayloft.

My mother fixed up a plate of spaghetti and told me to take it to him. I grabbed his schoolbooks. And when my father wasn't looking, I took the flashlight.

I thought I should have brought a cold rag and some ice when I handed up the plate and other things to Dennis. His left eye was swollen almost shut.

Dennis was so mad at the old man, he said he was going to steal his Oldsmobile and drive Mom to Milwaukee. He planned on taking her to Odanah on the way—see her relatives, visit her parents' graves. Then they would stay with Aunt Sylvia in Milwaukee or with our oldest brother, Frankie, because he had moved into a bigger apartment. Mom would get her dishwashing job back at the restaurant, and Dennis would go back to Division High School.

"What about your summer jobs program?" I ask. "Aren't you supposed to work for the forestry department?"

"Trimming trees? Clearing brush? Spending my whole summer in the sticks?"

But then I asked him about Robert. He would go with them, and so would Philly. I didn't ask him about the rest of us. Dennis finished the last bite of his spaghetti, put his hand on his sore eye, and sat back against the hay. He told me to take the flashlight. "Mom's going to need it when she takes Whiskey out before going to bed."

I stuck the flashlight in my front pants pocket and slid to the ladder. But Dennis sat up and said one more thing. "Don't worry about Mom. She'll be fine once she can see her sisters and Frankie again this summer. A couple weeks with Aunt Sylvia and the other sisters, laughing and carrying on like they do—that'll last her a long time, until next year when she can go back again. And you never know. Maybe Mom will get the old man committed to a hospital so he can dry out and get his head examined—realize once and for all that he is not a farmer and never will be. I'll tell you something else. If Mom ever does get him committed, she can get his monthly veterans disability check. Then we all can move back to Milwaukee."

※[ ]※

There are only two weeks left before the end of school, but it may be forever before my mother gets her chance to visit her sisters. My father was drinking again last night. He's pretty easy to knock down when he's drunk. And that's what Dennis and Joseph did. They pushed him down and dragged him out to the chicken coop to sleep with the chickens.

My mother told my brothers to find out how much money he blew at the bar. They searched his pockets and found a handful of change. There was nothing in the old man's wallet. Dennis asked my mom if they could keep the change and go to town to play pool.

They must have stayed overnight at a friend's house, maybe at Dale Olson's place.

My mother is silent again this morning. She stares off while standing over a boiling pot of water with a box of oatmeal in her hands.

Philly is tucking in Robert, who is asleep on the couch. Scott, Michael, and I are sitting at the kitchen table, fighting over a clean bowl and spoon. Scott keeps asking when the oatmeal is going to be done. He already has a new stick of margarine opened.

From the window, my sister spots the bus turning off the highway. Scott says we're going to have to go without eating again. He reaches in his pocket and asks if I have my free lunch ticket.

Philly and the others rush to the door, but I stay at the table.

"Come on!" my sister yells at me. "The bus isn't gonna wait all day!"

"I can't go to school!"

"You have to go to school if you want to pass the second grade!"

"I have to talk to Mom, so quit telling me what to do!"

Scott leaves the front door open. I feel the cold, sunny air rushing inside, blasting my bare feet. I get up to close the door and look out, seeing Whiskey wagging his tail as my sister and brother get on the bus. The bus driver honks his horn. I look at my shoes on the floor, covered with dry mud. I reach in my pocket, both pockets. I can't find my free lunch ticket. The horn honks again and again, but I don't move. I can't even close the front door, which I should do because I'm afraid my mother is going to hear that horn and snap out of it. I know she is going to threaten me with the broom if I don't get a move on.

But I can't go to school. I don't think I can ever go back. I want to tell my mother why I can't go to school. I want to tell her that I'm flunking in this new, stupid school. I want to tell her that someone needs to talk to my teacher, Mrs. Schmidt, about her stupid writing on the chalkboards. She writes down numbers, then makes huge white letters on that chalkboard, all of them twisting and swirling around like a messy spider web. I want my mother to go in and sit down with Mrs. Schmidt and tell her that back at Lincoln Avenue Elementary in Milwaukee, they never taught us how to write beautiful like she does in her letters, beautiful like the nuns used to write when she was going to school at St. Mary's. I want to tell my mother to just stop and listen to me for once. Just snap out of it and turn off that boiling pot of oatmeal water before she burns the whole garage down!

Suddenly my mother glares at me. I hear the bus driving off, but all I can do is wipe my eyes with my cold hands.

"Close that damn door!" she yells. "What the hell's the matter with you? We can't heat the outside."

"I can't go to school!" I tell her. "I can't understand a word she writes!"

"Who?"

"Mrs. Schmidt! She says she's gonna hold me back a year if I don't start reading her writing on the chalkboard!"

Suddenly Robert begins crying. "Now look what you've done with all your damn screaming," my mother says as she turns the stove burner off.

I close the door and watch my mother picking up the baby in her arms. She sits with him in a kitchen chair. She slips her dress down.

Robert's cries turn to sucking noises. My mother reaches for her cold cup of coffee and asks me who pissed the bed last night. "Was it you?"

"No! That was Michael."

"Well, somebody's gotta clean up that stink."

"I'm not doing it. Michael's the one who did it, not me."

"I guess maybe it's time for the broom then."

I offer to start on the dishes instead. She says she will think about it, but first she wants me to get her writing pad and Bic pens.

"You don't have any paper or pens left," I say. "That Philly. She took 'em, not me."

My mother looks at Robert. I reach for my own notebook on the edge of the table. I wait until she looks at me again, and then I bring it to her. My mother tells me to go into the bathroom. "On top of the medicine cabinet there should be a new Bic pen."

I do as she tells me. When I return, she is flipping through my notebook, flipping pages of Spider-Man and Daredevil drawings. My mother tells me to pull a chair next to her. I ask her if she's going to write to one of her sisters.

She shrugs. "Oh, I don't know. I might write to your Aunt Sylvia." And then she writes in my notebook. "See? This is how you make a *D*."

She gives me the pen, and she guides my fingers with hers. We do this until we get to the end of "Dear Sylvia," then she takes the pen and writes more.

"What are you going to write to her, Mom?"

"Her knee. She was supposed to have surgery a few weeks ago."

"You mean from that night when she slipped on the ice at the bottom of our porch?"

My mother smiles.

"Someone called the ambulance," I say. "But she didn't want to go to the hospital, did she?"

My mother covers her mouth as she bursts into laughter.

"It was New Year's Eve," she says, trying to catch her breath. "She wouldn't let that ambulance driver talk her into going into the emergency room because she was afraid Philomena and Victoria were gonna drink up the rest of the beer."

"And remember that guy Mitchie?"

"Your Aunt Victoria's son."

"Yeah, he got all drunk at that wedding party and started dancing, crashing into a bunch of chairs and stuff."

"Mitchie wanted me to dance with him to a Glenn Miller song he played on the jukebox. But I said, 'Oh, come on now! Leave me be, Mitchie.'"

Suddenly my mother's laughter turns to a sigh. She lets me take the pen while she switches breasts for the baby.

"He died, didn't he, Mom?"

She only nods and tells me to go get her purse sitting on the kitchen windowsill. I know what's in that black purse—coupons, her fake silver earrings, lipstick, a handful of pennies, and a letter she got from Aunt Victoria last week. My mother unsnaps her purse and unfolds that letter. She spreads it out on the table next to the notebook. She likes to read as she writes.

She picks up her pen and tells me she has to think now. I leave the table and head for the bedroom before she remembers that I am supposed to do the dishes.

I don't tell my mother, but I know what's in that letter. Dennis read it to us. Mitchie was at a bar downtown, on Wisconsin Avenue. He went home with a guy who lived above a George Webb Restaurant on Cherry Street.

. . . I guess they got to drinking too much, and things must have gotten out of hand. The cops said that guy went nuts with a bat. Mitchie was twenty-eight. I know you can't make it, but we're gonna drive up to Odanah for the wake. We'll bury him next to mother at the tribal ceme- tery. We'll have a feast, of course. I suppose we'll get to drinking and telling stories about Mitchie. You know how Sylvia and Philomena are. They can't stop once they get going telling stories we all thought we had forgotten . . .

By the time I am almost done reading through all of Joseph's new comic books, I hear the school bus squealing its brakes at the edge of the driveway. I quickly stuff the comics back under the bed and run out of the bedroom.

My mother is still sitting at the kitchen table, listening to the radio as she writes. Pages of her letters are scattered in front of her. She goes over each page, writing more on each side. She gets up and reaches for the cold coffeepot on the stove. Suddenly an old song comes on the radio. It's an old-time dancing song. But my mother does not dance. She only smiles and stares at the radio. Then she reaches for my notebook again and turns to a new page.

ᛞ[6]ᛢ

Dead Hippie Praying

Once we move into the farmhouse (maybe in a few weeks), my father says some things will stay the same. My mother will never have enough water to wash all the clothes. "The well's only twenty feet deep," he says, leaning against the new double sink in the kitchen. "We're going to have to keep hauling water from town for a long time to come."

My mother steps around Scott and me as we sit on the floor, scraping away old linoleum. I notice her snakes, the burn scars wrapped around her legs. "That water barrel's almost empty," she says. "I've scrubbed just about every damn floor in this house. Don't bother refilling it. I'm too worn out to be washing and hanging clothes today."

She goes into the living room to her mop and bucket. The sun is still shining through the brand-new picture window. The sun has stared through that window since this morning when we started ripping up the old kitchen floor. My mother wrings her mop one more time, then wipes dripping sweat from her face. "I need to get supper going," she says.

"We'll go to the Laundromat in the morning," my father says as she leaves through the back door.

Scott and I pretend to keep scraping, waiting until our father goes down to the basement to check on the sump pump. When he's gone, we race upstairs to find Dennis and Joseph. They already moved into one of the bedrooms a few days ago. We haven't seen the inside of their room yet, but Scott is pretty sure he knows where Joseph hides his comic books—in the bottom drawer. They found a dresser and an RCA hi-fi record player at the dump.

We see their muddy rubber boots and garden gloves in the hallway outside their room. The door is open, but we don't hear their music playing.

"It's fried," Dennis says as he pulls out the hi-fi speaker wires.

Joseph is stretched out on the bed with a comic book. "It was working fine last night," he says. And then he looks at Scott and me. "Have you guys been messing around in here?"

"No, it's the wiring," Dennis says. "You know people throw shit away for a reason." He kicks the hi-fi. It crashes against the wall.

"Hey!" Joseph says, reaching for an album cover on top of one of the speakers. "I hope you took off that Morrison LP."

"Who cares? The album's a piece of shit, too," Dennis says. He kicks it again, making sure the record player cracks in a hundred pieces.

"Yeah, but it's Dale Olson's shitty album, not ours," Joseph says as we watch pieces of the record twirl on the floor.

"I'll buy him a new one when I get paid from my job this summer."

"Why is it a piece of shit?" I ask.

"He just talks, doesn't sing. Thinks he's a poet, I guess. He's got one song, if you can call it that, where he talks about seeing some dead Indians on a highway. That's supposed to be profound?"

I shrug my shoulders and stare at the white walls covered with magic marker. Joseph has started drawing life-size comic book heroes on the walls—Spider-Man, Captain America, and the Scarlet Witch. Joseph looks at Scott and me. "Hey, you guys. I'll let you read the new Avengers comic if you go get the radio in the garage."

"You get it," I say.

"I've been pulling weeds all day. Come on."

"What do you think we've been doing?"

Joseph holds up his new Avengers comic. "The Wasp's boobs are bigger," he says with a grin.

Dennis laughs, reaching for the comic. "Hey, ever wonder why the Vision's skin is red?"

"It's not skin," Scott says. "He's an android."

"Yeah, an Indian android," Dennis says. "It makes complete sense. You know how he always feels inferior around the white super-heroes, wishes he was human? Well, that's the way white people make Indians feel—make them think being human is the same as being white."

"I don't know what he's whining about," Joseph says, taking his comic back. "He could have the Scarlet Witch any day, or the Wasp for that matter."

I sit on the edge of the bed and lean over, hoping to get a look at the Wasp's new boobs. "You think that's why Mom married the old man?" I say to Dennis. "She wanted to be white?"

Dennis laughs again, then grabs one of the broken wood pieces of the hi-fi record player. He turns over a dented metal garbage can and sits on the chair next to it with the piece of broken wood in his hand. He bangs away, looking at the Scarlet Witch drawing on the wall. Then he sings to her in a powwow voice.

Hey-ya! Hey-ya! Hey-ya! I say!
I'll get down with you!
Hey-ya! Hey-ya! Hey-ya! I say!

They don't have powwows in Big Falls. We're the only Indians living here.

Back in Milwaukee, my mother used to go to powwows in one of the parks with her sisters. Dennis says he heard from friends in high school that they've got powwows at Red Lake and Nett Lake during the summer. But my mother doesn't say anything, and Dennis changes the subject.

⋇[ ]⋇

My mother fries hamburgers, and Whiskey sits by the stove, looking up at her, sniffing at the smell. Philly stands next to her, opening cans of kidney beans and tomato paste. My sister asks when the rest of us can move into the farmhouse. My mother only glances back at my father, who is watching the Canadian news on the television. The only time he watches the news is when he's not drinking.

The rest of us sort through dirty clothes, shoving them in pillowcases and two laundry baskets. We make Michael pick up the clothes that are still wet from his peeing in bed at night.

During supper, my mother is always the last to eat. But tonight she is eating slower than usual. After we clear our plates, Philly tells her that she shouldn't have to do dishes because she helped cook. My mother looks at me. I glare at my sister.

"Philly hasn't done dishes in a week!" I say. "Anybody can open a stupid can of kidney beans!"

But my mother just sits at the table, looking at me. Finally she dips a piece of bread in her bowl.

"Want me to get the broom, Mom?" Philly says.

"Shut up!" I say.

But my mother still says nothing. When she finishes eating, she gets up and takes her bowl to the sink. She turns on the faucet, then scoops out some Oxydol from the box and pours it in the dishwater. She tells Philly and John to start hauling the laundry out to the Oldsmobile. She leans against the sink and rubs the back of her neck. She stands for a few more long seconds, then reaches for some dirty dishes. I see the tear in the side of her dress is bigger. I look down and stare at her snake scars around her calves and ankles. And then I reach for the towel. I stand next to my mother, waiting for her to dip dishes in the rinse water. My mother says nothing, and neither do I. We just stand there together, her arm sometimes touching the side of my face.

>[ ]<

I am the first one up the next morning. My mother is sitting at the kitchen table, rocking Robert in her arms. My father finishes the last of his coffee, then slides a pile of quarters off the table and into a brown bag. He says if I want to go with them and help my mother out with the laundry, I should find my shoes.

My mother takes Robert into the bedroom and lays him next to Philly. She puts on her sweater, and I follow her out the front door.

Even though it's early June, the grass sparkles with frost under the blue-sky sun. The chickens wander around the yard, picking at the white blades of grass. I put my chin under my T-shirt and blow steamy breath on my chest, and then I squeeze up against the laundry in the back of my father's Oldsmobile.

My father turns on the heater, and I lick the frost from the window. The frost is thicker in the shadows of the woods as we drive along the dirt road. It looks almost like an inch of new snow on the pine branches. My father tells my mother that he's glad he didn't start planting the garden yet. "It'll probably freeze tonight as well," he says.

When we reach the highway, the Oldsmobile comes to a complete stop. My father points at something on the pavement. "What in the hell is that?"

I roll the window down all the way and wait for my cloudy breath to drift away. And then I see him, a white hippie with long black hair stretched out on his back in the middle of Highway 71. He has his hands folded together on his chest. He's wearing a buckskin jacket, and his white jeans are tucked inside leather boots.

"You think he's dead?" my father says.

"You better go see before one of those big logging trucks runs him over," my mother says.

My father puts the Oldsmobile in park and reaches for his door handle. "Maybe he's on a vision quest," he says, smiling.

My mother covers her mouth and laughs a little, then twists the rearview mirror. She starts fixing the bobby pins in her hair.

I lean out the window. My father slowly walks to the hippie, then around him. Finally my father kicks at the hippie's boot. The hippie slowly sits up with a grin on his face.

I can't hear what they're saying to each other, but my father points toward Big Falls. The hippie shakes his head and looks in the other direction. I ask my mother what a vision quest is, even though I know she's not going to tell me much about it.

"It's an old Indian ceremony, something you're supposed to do in the woods, not in the middle of the highway."

My father puts out his hand to help the hippie get up, but the hippie shakes his head no. He gets up on his own and smiles at my dad, then staggers down the highway toward Bemidji.

"I guess he got tired of hitchhiking and figured someone was bound to pick him up if he laid in the middle of the road," my father says as he shifts the Oldsmobile. We turn on the highway, and I look at that hippie one more time.

Just when we hit the Big Falls city limits sign, we spot a black 1950s car loaded with Indians coming out of nowhere. My father eases up on the gas pedal and gives them as much of the road as he can. He stops his Oldsmobile on the side of the highway. My mother turns her face to the window. I know she doesn't want the Indians to spot her. She's afraid they'll pull over and ask to come by the farm for fried potatoes, scrambled eggs, and bread, then crack open their beer cans and tell laughing stories about each other and the other Chippewas who live in these parts. And then they'll have to spend the night and another night.

Dennis once told me my mother quit drinking long before I was born, that she didn't care for the taste of it. She doesn't mind it when her sisters drink, but that's because they always go home when they're done.

But the Indians do not stop. I can't tell how many are in the car as they whiz by, but I can see a man and woman in the front seat, laughing and singing.

My father glances one more time in his side mirror and smiles. "Look how fast they're moving," he says. "I hope that hippie didn't go back to sleep."

"Get back on the road now," my mother says. "That Laundromat's gonna get more crowded the longer we sit out here in the sticks."

But there's only one lady in the Laundromat when we bring in the clothes. She squints to avoid the smoke from the long, thin cigarette hanging out of her mouth as she pulls out clothes from a dryer and sets them on the counter. I think each of her arms and legs is as skinny as her cigarette.

The lady nods at my mother as she blows a cloud of smoke above her short red hair. My mother looks down, smiles like she always does when she meets new people in town.

"Cold as a witch's tit out, isn't it?" the lady says to my mother.

My mother nods and tells me to get the Oxydol before my father drives off to the post office. When I get back inside the Laundromat, the lady is helping my mother load clothes in the machines.

"I had to get a fire going last night only to find out I was outta wood—hi, name's Kathy Johns—good to meet you—so there I am outside in my parka and pajamas splitting wood, and all of a sudden I see these goddamned owl eyes glowing at me in the trees—where you from, honey? Milwaukee? I was born and raised in Big Falls—all ten of us make a living here, except for one—Denice, the youngest, lives in the Cities—I hate owls—God, am I afraid of owls—they say an owl is a sign of death—you the folks living out at the old Peterson home?—I think they moved to Bemidji after that fire— this is a one-fire-truck town—we got two cafes—the Sportsman's, they make the best food in my opinion—Janie, cooks a steak more tender than any fancy restaurant in Bemidji, let me tell you . . ."

"We saw a hippie sleeping in the middle of the highway," I say.

"Now, don't get me wrong. Thompson's Red Owl is great for running in to get milk and a loaf of bread," Kathy Johns says. "But I hope you're doing your big shopping at the Piggly Wiggly in the Falls—International Falls."

"We thought he was dead," I say.

"What's that, honey? You saw a hippie on the highway? You're gonna see a lot more this summer. They come up from the Cities to commune with nature, I guess. A lot of them hang out down at the old Bible camp along the river."

My mother calls me with the nodding of her head. I start dropping quarters in the machines. But one of the doors won't close for my mother. Kathy Johns puts out her cigarette and shakes her head. "You gotta get mean with these sons-a-bitches, honey." And then she raises her skinny leg and kicks the machine door until it locks.

"Listen, honey, I gotta head out. We got big doings next month on the Fourth—parade, fireworks," Kathy Johns says to me as she lights up another cigarette, then puts on her red and black checkered coat. She picks up her laundry basket and moves to the glass door. "The ladies from the church sell hot dogs and pop—you kids'll love it."

She races out the door, and I watch her climb into her blue pickup truck. Exhaust blows into the sunlight as she peels out of the gravel parking lot and onto Main Street.

I ask my mother if we can go to the Fourth of July celebration.

She says nothing as she counts out the last of her quarters.

>[ ]<

My mother wants to drive down by the river, see some other part of Big Falls besides the post office and Hagen's Corner Bar. I tell my father I want to see this Bible camp where the hippies hang out.

Highway 71 crosses north over the Big Fork River. Right under the bridge is where the rapids begin to form—flowing brown water turns to white when it splashes against huge gray rocks. My father parks his Oldsmobile. The three of us stand at the edge of the river. My father tells me not to get too close. He says if you stare into the fast-moving water you can get dizzy and fall in.

I am walking back to the Oldsmobile with my mother when a forest ranger pulls up in a green truck. My father rolls a cigarette and starts talking to the ranger.

I open a bag of red licorice from the Red Owl grocery bags filled with powdered milk, yeast, buttermilk, brown sugar, lard, oatmeal, and two pounds of hamburger. My mother pulls down the mirror in front of her and asks me if she has too much gray hair in the back of her head. I say no as I look into the woods that surround the campgrounds.

"I don't want you kids swimming near those rapids this summer," she says. I nod and spot a huge, rusting metal barrel on the edge of the park. It's turned on its side. The front part is cut out, and it has a gate of bars on top like a guillotine blade ready to come slamming down. I ask my mother to look.

"I have no idea what that is," she says.

"Looks like a cage."

"Maybe it's for those hippies," she says.

"Why do you think that hippie came to Big Falls? What does *commune* mean? You think Kathy Johns is right when she said he wanted to commune with nature?"

My mother tells me to stop asking so many questions and to make sure I divide up the rest of the licorice for my brothers and sister. I shove two extra pieces in my pocket before putting the rest back in the grocery bag.

When my father swings his Oldsmobile around so we can see that barrel up close, he tells my mother it's a bear trap, that the forest ranger told him it's rare to spot bears in the park so early in the summer, that there's no garbage scraps for the bear to eat with no campers around. My mother rolls up her window and tells my father to speed up. He takes his time, barely moving forward. "Oh, for Pete's sake, Don! Let's get the hell outta here before that thing sees us."

"What'll they do to that bear once they catch him?" I ask.

"Kill it, I hope," my mother says.

"Nah, they'll take it out deeper into the woods and let it go," my father says. "The strawberries will be coming out in a few weeks and then the blueberries. That black bear will have plenty to eat. He'll forget all about this park."

I catch a good look at a chunk of bloody meat dangling in front of the open end of the barrel. I sometimes see faces in things if I stare long enough. I think about that hippie and that Indian car. I wonder if when we get close to home we'll see that hippie's bloody face on the highway.

My mother snaps at my father again. He jerks the car into gear, and we head back up to Highway 71.

When we make our turn off the highway toward home, I look for the bloody hippie. But there is no sign of him or his dead face on the side of the highway.

⟨[7]⟩

Wild Trees

A row of smaller pine trees, four of them reaching just above the first-floor windows of the farmhouse, stands in the front yard, facing the sun. Their long, thick branches are so heavy they touch the Earth.

I think they are my mother's favorite trees. Not because she likes to sit and stare at them from the big living room picture window in the farmhouse, but because she can hide beneath their blanket of branches when my father comes home drunk, when she's not in the mood to argue with the old man about how everything that's going wrong is her fault.

In the mornings when the old man is still sleeping from being drunk all night, my mother asks me to walk into town with Whiskey to pick up the mail. Some mornings I tell her to just ask Dennis to get up and drive the old man's Oldsmobile into town. But then I remember he gets up earlier than me for his summer forestry job. I usually shrug when she asks me if I'll go into town for her. Then she tells me to go in the basement and look behind the shelves under the stairs. "There's a plastic bag of cinnamon rolls hidden behind some cans of tomato sauce. You can have one if you go."

But this morning my father is not sleeping off his drunk. He is in the barn, shoveling out old, dried manure to make room for the new Holsteins he plans to buy. My mother is in the kitchen making her bread. All of her pans are neatly placed on the brand-new shelves beneath the counter. When she turns her back, mixing flour into the big bowl of foaming yeast with her hands, I stick my mouth under the faucet for a quick drink.

"There are clean cups in the dish drain," she says.

"I didn't see them. Sorry."

I cringe, waiting for her hand to come and smack me across the head. But instead my mother tells me to reach in her dress pocket and pull out some change. "If you get the mail, you can have what's in there." I count out seventy-five cents.

"Now, listen closely," she says as she pulls sticky dough from her fingers. "I'm expecting an important letter."

"What kind of letter?"

"Bad River." My mother wipes her forehead with the back of her hand and asks me if I can keep a secret. "The tribe is gonna be sending out a land payment. I need to fill out a form and send it back."

"How much money?"

She glares at me, and I squeeze the quarters in my hand. "I don't want you saying a word about that letter," she orders. "Just shove it in your pocket and come right home."

Whiskey and I take the train tracks. I walk along the iron rails, balancing for as long as I can. Every few seconds, Whiskey dashes off into the ditch, chasing after birds or grasshoppers. He never wanders off too far into the woods because I call out to him. I don't trust the woods. I don't like to think about what's in those woods. Thinking about other things makes me feel safer.

Mrs. Schmidt told Mom that she would pass me into the third grade on the condition that I practice my cursive writing and that I do all the assignments in my math workbook this summer. I haven't even opened that workbook. But I might not have to. I just know they'll let me in the third grade if we can move back to Milwaukee. I'm hoping Mom can get enough money from her Indian payment and take all of us back with her, including Whiskey.

I don't think Whiskey remembers when we lived upstairs in that rented house in Milwaukee. I hope we don't move there again, but I hope we'll live near Lincoln Avenue Elementary again. With that Indian payment, I hope we get all-new furniture and new clothes. I won't have to hang around that stupid Ronnie Gibbs anymore because I won't be wearing the same kind of Salvation Army shirts and shoes he always wears. Maybe Mom will even have one of those Tupperware parties she likes to go to—have one where we invite all her sisters and their friends over for cookies and Kool-Aid. Of course, the best part will be not having the social workers coming by with boxes of oatmeal and powdered milk. And after Christmas, I won't have to make up getting presents. I can just be the first one with his hand up in Mrs. Baker's class to tell everyone about all the toys and new clothes I got.

Once we get into town, the first place we go straight to is the Red Owl. I have enough for a Shasta root beer and some baked beans candy, which I share with Whiskey. We cross Main Street to the post office. I tell Whiskey that I'll be right back. I decide I'm going to put my mother's letter from the tribe against the post office window by the sun and see if I can read through the envelope how much they're going to send her.

But there is no letter from the tribe. The only thing Butch Miller, the postman, hands me is another catalog for ordering seeds and a little envelope with my name on it, an invitation for Mike Hovan's ninth birthday party. I count out the rest of the change my mother gave me—only twenty cents, not enough even to buy a birthday card. I read the invitation again: *Outdoor Barbeque and Fun and Games, Noon—4:00 PM.* I decide to head back home because I don't even know Mike Hovan that well, anyway.

Whiskey and I only get to the edge of town, just past the Mission Covenant Church, when I hear Mike Hovan's voice yelling for me. He's coming up behind me, riding a brand-new ten-speed. He yells again, then squeezes the brakes on the handlebar and spins in front of me, making a tire mark on the pavement.

"You're coming to my party, right?" Mike says as he takes out a pack of Old Gold cigarettes from his front shirt pocket. He slips one between his lips and sticks the open pack toward me. "Want one?"

I look around the empty street and tell him that maybe he should put it away in case the cop drives by.

"Loken? The hell with him," he says. And then he makes a fist and shakes it, laughing. "If he tries to tell me what I can and can't do, I'll kick his ass."

"What about your dad?" I ask as he lights his cigarette without inhaling.

"He'll kick his ass, too!"

"Your dad lets you smoke?"

"Hell, yeah! I've been smoking since I was six."

Mike lifts the back of his bike and spins the tire. "Let's head over to my place."

I tell him that I only got his invitation today, that I didn't have time to get a present. But Mike tells me he would rather have nothing than what he'll probably get from those dumbass twins, Rick and Robbie.

"You don't like playing Monopoly?" I ask.

"I already have that retarded game, and Yahtzee and Chinese checkers. Now, come on. Let's go back to my place."

Some of the streets in Big Falls are still gravel. I walk along with Whiskey while Mike speeds up and slams on his bike brakes, kicking up dust. He tells me that what he really would like for his birthday is a six-pack of beer. "And not that Hamm's crap," he says. "I only drink Schmidt."

Mike's dad drives a chip truck, hauling wood chips from the sawmill up to the Boise Cascade plant in International Falls. He says his mom and dad meet up at Hagen's Corner Bar after work for supper. Usually there's a casserole or TV dinners in the oven when he gets home from school. Mike can't wait until he turns sixteen, gets his driver's license, and quits school to go to work in the woods with his Uncle Frank. "I already know how to drive a skidder and run a chainsaw," he says.

Whiskey stays on the porch, and Mike and I take off our shoes before going inside. The floors are covered in spongy, brown shag carpeting. There are matching lamps built right into the little matching tables on each end of the couch. They have bluebirds painted on their shades. Mike screams for his mom as he goes into the kitchen. I stare at the color television screen that no one is watching. I haven't watched *Scooby Doo* since we moved to Big Falls. They don't show American cartoons on Canadian TV. I quickly sit down on the couch as I hear some yelling coming from the kitchen. "Why in the hell are you bringing over friends when the party doesn't start until noon?!"

Mike returns with two bottles of Coke and tells me to follow him upstairs. He shares a bedroom with his older brother, Jimmy. His two older sisters have rooms to themselves. We sit on the bottom bunk. Mike has magazine pictures of Arctic Cat snowmobiles on his paneled walls and a fishing pole next to his dresser. He slides a red metal locker from under the bed and begins spinning the combination lock. "You ever have rum and Coke?" he asks.

"What is it?"

"Get a whiff of this," he says as he unscrews a bottle lid and holds it under my nose. "Jimmy got it for me."

I look away and tell Mike that once in a while I sip some of the foam from my dad's Pabst beer after he shakes some salt on it. "When he's not looking."

I watch as he carefully pours some rum in his Coke bottle. He takes a swig and pours in more. He offers me the bottle, but I tell him I only like the taste of Pabst.

In the garage, Mike shows me the new Arctic Cat. He pulls back the plastic cover and sits on the shiny black and purple snowmobile, pretending to drive. "So what do you think of Melissa Russell?" he asks. "You know the tall redhead in class?"

"Is she coming to your party?"

"Melissa and I are gonna disappear for a while once she gets here," he says, lighting up another Old Gold cigarette. "Sure you don't even wanna drag of this?"

I nod and take the cigarette. I start coughing, and then my head gets dizzy. Mike tells me to hold onto the cigarette while he takes a snort from his rum bottle. Suddenly the garage door opens. I drop the cigarette, and Mike slips the bottle under his shirt. But it's too late. His mother, her hair still in curlers and her pointy glasses glaring in the sunlight, reaches for a tennis racket hanging on a nail on the wall. She screams and races after Mike. I run in the other direction toward the open door.

Whiskey and I sit on the grass in the backyard. We hear the sound of pots and pans banging and more yelling coming from the house. "Just you wait until I tell your father! Just you wait, kiddo!" A door slams, then I hear the sound of a car starting up and squealing out of the driveway. I look at the silent house. Finally Mike comes out with two plates of chocolate cake and vanilla ice cream. He has a red streak across the left side of his freckled face. His eyes are blurry. We sit at a picnic bench. Mike says nothing. I finish eating, then look at his melting ice cream.

"Did your mom go somewhere?" I ask.

"She's up at the bar with my dad," he whispers. "You're not gonna leave, are you? Nita, my sister, should be back soon. She'll fire up the grill." And then Mike starts laughing. "Come on! Stay! It'll be a lot more fun without my mom screaming at everyone."

But Nita screams as much as Mike's mom. When the Bloom twins, Rick and Robbie, show up, Nita shoves a plate of burnt hamburgers on the picnic table and wants to know "just who in the hell ate some of that damn birthday cake!" Mike tells her to "kiss off." She tells him he can "light his own damn candles!" The twins start laughing as they pass around the buns and chips. I tear my hamburger in two and sneak half to Whiskey.

Nita calms down some when she lights up a cigarette and sits on the edge of the table. Her hair is as blond and short as Mike's. Nita sticks her cigarette pack under her T-shirt sleeve, rolling it up above her muscles. I glance at her blue jeans, notice her cowboy boots and the thick leather watchband on her right wrist. "So what else you guys wanna do?" she says. "But make it quick. I got softball practice in twenty minutes. Who wants cake? Why don't you little shits eat some cake?"

Mike doesn't like playing sports, which is why we probably never got to be good friends in school. He didn't have to play football or even kickball during phy ed because he got his mom to write him a note saying he had asthma. When we finish the cake and wait for

Mike to open his present from the twins, Robbie asks me if I want to play football at school. Mike rips only half of the gift wrapping away, just enough to see it's a board game, Battleship.

I reach down and pet Whiskey. He looks at me with his big eyes. I know he wants to leave as much as me. Rick and Robbie get up with their paper plates and move to the trash can by the grill. Mike asks me, starts begging me to stay longer. "Let's have another cigarette and get drunk, okay? Then we'll head over to Melissa Russell's place. She lives in the trailer park with her mom. Her mom is working at the gas station tonight. You can make out with her, too. What do you say?"

>[ ]<

Rick and Robbie get along for most of the afternoon at the playground until Robbie gets tackled hard. He jumps up and throws the football at his brother's head. And then the wrestling begins, like it always does until one of them starts crying, usually Robbie. Rick calls his brother a bawl baby, then apologizes, even suggests we play tag football instead. But Robbie is already climbing over the fence. Rick says he'd better go because if he doesn't, Robbie will make up some lie to their parents about getting picked on, and he'd better be there to defend himself.

When Whiskey and I get uptown, I spot my father's Oldsmobile parked in front of Municipal Liquors. Sometimes my father will go in there instead of Hagen's Corner Bar. Kids are not allowed inside Municipal Liquors. I think about sitting in the backseat of my father's Oldsmobile but realize Whiskey and I would probably be stuck there, waiting forever. And by the time I got sick of waiting around for the old man, it would be too dark to walk home.

I check to see where the sun is at in the sky. Even though the clouds make it darker than it is, I tell Whiskey we have plenty of time to make it home. We walk along the highway just in case my father does decide to leave the bar early. I have to stop and take some deep breaths because I feel like I might throw up. I can still smell Mike Hovan's rum and Coke. After I open my eyes, I look around for Whiskey. He's staring across the ditch. The hair on his back is standing straight up. He barks, and I hear something growl back. I look over my shoulder to the edge of the woods. There, in an open patch of tall grass, a black bear turns, glares, and growls at me. I slowly walk sideways to Whiskey, hoping he stays there long enough for me to wrap my arms around his neck. I keep my eyes on the bear as I reach for Whiskey. The second I grab the dog, the black bear rears up on his back legs, standing, growling at me even louder. Whiskey barks and squirms, trying to break free. But I hold on, not taking my eyes off that black bear. The bear growls one more time, then falls back on all four of his legs. He twists his head and runs off into the woods. I hold Whiskey until he stops barking. When I am sure the woods are quiet again, I jump up. I call Whiskey as I run as fast as I can down the highway toward home.

When we make the turn on the dirt road and I can see the house, I slow down. I put my hands on my knees and lower my head to throw up, chocolate cake and burnt hamburger pieces splashing against the gravel between my feet. I spit a few more times and start walking, following Whiskey the rest of the way home.

My mother is already getting ready for bed when we reach the house. I see her carrying a can of bug spray. Scott and Michael follow, carrying pillows and a blanket. They head to the row of smaller pine trees in the front yard. Philly comes out of the house, walking slowly with Robert, holding his hand.

I don't dare tell my mother about the black bear because I know she'll get scared and decide she has to sleep in the house. She'll have to put up with the old man's drunk arguing. And I don't think I can ever tell her because she may end up being scared of black bears forever.

There's never enough room for me under the tree. I turn on my side with my head under the tips of the pine branches and stare at my mother. She sprays the rest of the OFF! on her arms and begins rubbing it in, around her face and neck as well. She doesn't ask me about her Indian payment letter. She only tells me that as soon as we hear the old man's Oldsmobile coming up the driveway, I'm going to have to go hide someplace else.

Philly asks if she should go get our mother's new Reader's Digest book, the one Irene Cloutier gave her today when she visited. Irene and her husband Hank come by at least once a week. Sometimes they bring leftover clothes and books from rummage sales. When my father is not drinking, he and Hank walk around the garden and talk. Irene always stays in the car. My mother leans against the side of their Buick and listens to Irene's stories about who's always at the bar every night drinking, who's "shacking up" with who, and how people in Big Falls are always wanting to know other people's business.

Irene and Hank have only one child. Irene says Hank used to be a "real big-time boozer" until a few years ago. She says her husband finally sobered up after their daughter, Linda, almost died in a car accident. Hank was driving Linda home from cheerleading practice when a deer jumped in front of the car. Besides the broken ribs and leg, Linda had to have her jaw wired up for months.

I ask my mother what new Reader's Digest book Irene brought over today, if she could read out loud to us. But she shakes her head and tells Philly not to bother going in the house to get it. There is not enough light underneath the pines. Instead, my mother swirls her fingertip in the air.

"Who are you writing to, Mom?" Philly asks.

"No one in particular," my mother says. "Actually, now I'm writing out a list of things I'll need to buy."

"Once you get your Indian payment check?" I say.

Philly sticks her elbow in my arm. "How do you know about that check?" she asks. "I'm the only one Mom told, not you!"

I want to tell my sister off, but I know if we get to arguing, pushing and shoving, my mother will tell me to go inside the house. So I just glare at Philly and ask our mother what she plans on buying with her Indian check.

"I want a car."

"You can't drive," my sister says.

"Yes, I can. It's not hard to learn," she says with a laugh.

"You gonna drive back to Milwaukee?" I ask.

"Maybe. Maybe Chicago or New York." And then my mother laughs again. "Maybe I'll drive to Paris."

"Paris?" my sister says. "You're gonna have to buy a boat, Mom."

I look up into the skies, seeing the clouds covering up the sun. The wind picks up. My mother tells us if it starts raining, we're all going to have to go inside. Suddenly it gets quiet under the tree. And then I hear my sister whispering, asking my mother to tell her more about growing up on the reservation at Odanah. But like always, my mother does not say much about Bad River—the swamps, mosquitoes, the cold Lake Superior, and how easy it was to get lost in the woods.

I ask my mother if the trees at Bad River were like the ones up here. She whispers to me, telling me to lower my voice.

"Well, are they the same?" I ask.

"No. The woods at Bad River are bigger, darker."

"Are the trees wild?" I ask.

I listen for my mother's voice, but there is only silence. I close my eyes and drift off.

I feel a drop of rain fall on my cheek, then another. It's dark now. I sit up and see my father's Oldsmobile parked in the driveway under the yard light. The kitchen light is on. Suddenly Scott scoots out from under the tree and asks if I want to go inside.

We slowly push open the kitchen door and see the old man sitting alone at the table with a cigarette that is burned down to his knuckles. His head is slumped, and he mumbles something about Milwaukee, about having to move away from my mother's nosy Indian sisters, the nosy cops, nosy social workers. Suddenly Whiskey gets between us and rushes inside to the old man. He reaches down and pets the dog. "Even those damned VA doctors couldn't mind their own business," he says to Whiskey. "Couldn't mind their own goddamned business when it came to my hardworking right to have a beer once in a while."

The rain falls harder, and we wait as long as we can until the old man finally stands up and staggers down the hall to the bathroom. We burst through the door, through the kitchen, and up the stairs.

John is the only one upstairs. He sits in the dark, holding the transistor radio, trying to get it to work. "Scott spilled Kool-Aid on it," I say as I reach out to pet Whiskey.

"No, I didn't! You did!"

"Keep your voices down," John says. "You want the old man coming up here?"

"Now what'll we do?" I ask. "No radio, can't watch TV, can't even turn on the light to read comics."

I sit on the floor, lean my arms on the windowsill, and look at the other pine trees, the taller ones between the front yard and dirt road. The yard light touches the ends of the pine needles, making the shadows beneath their branches even darker. The wind moves the trees, making them sway like they're getting ready to leave, to go back into the forests with the other wild trees.

I stare into the trees. I spot some glowing eyes staring back at me from deep inside those black, rainy pines. I want to stop looking, but I can't take my eyes away.

"Do you see that?" I whisper to my brothers. "There's a big bear hiding in that tree, that one over there. Maybe we should tell Mom, tell her to come in the house."

John tells me I should never stare too long at trees in the night. "You start seeing things you don't want to see, and before you know it, you're too scared to go to sleep. Now, get in bed and stop looking out the window."

I can't close my eyes. I feel Whiskey's warm head against my feet and stare at Joseph's Scarlet Witch comic drawing on the wall, waiting to see how bright red her cape, gloves, and boots are, when lightning flashes. I glance at my brothers' faces. Their eyes are closed. I tiptoe to the windowsill again and sit down. The bear's eyes are still glowing in the trees. Lightning flashes again, then a crash of thunder. I turn around to see if my brothers are still awake. I want to wake up Scott and tell him we need to warn Mom about the bear. But suddenly I'm no longer in the bedroom of the farmhouse. I'm in the middle of the woods, surrounded by pine trees. Where the door to the hall should be is now a path leading deeper into the forest. I look up and see the Scarlet Witch sitting in the trees. She has black fur for skin, long claws, and fangs. I can't move. She climbs down, never taking her eyes off me. I open my mouth, but I can't make any sounds. And then she comes to me, sniffing. She leans over me, and I can feel her hot, drippy breath on my face.

You should never stare into trees. They wear masks. They tell stories when they put on those masks—stories that will lead you so far into the woods you can lose your way back to the tamed world.

You will know you are lost when you realize these trees move, mostly the pines. They march through the meadows and on top of the hills, keeping watch over the land. They dance along the riverbank, splashing their big trunks to cool the sun's heat. They parade through the lowlands, carrying the dead to the gate that opens the path into the universe.

These trees protect sleeping birds and provide lodges for animal councils. And they tower to disguise what is left of an untouched garden, a sacred place where the seeds of creation, transformation, and rapture wait on their blooming, waiting until the world is a safe place again.

Wild trees don't like strangers. They think you bring fire. And you do.

You bring the fire because someone told you wild trees cannot hide when the skies spit burning streaks of white hot rage. Somewhere buried in your bundle is fire. You may not think you own it, but it's there. And when you realize your way is lost, when you feel the hard hide of wild trees pressing against you, wanting to know why you are in this place, fear will save you. You will reach inside your bundle and pull out that fire. You can flash the night into day with one swift strike against a rock. You can consume the Earth with your fire. And when you do, you can find your way again. It's a wide-open view now. Your fire has brought the Earth to its knees.

⟩[8]⟨

Evening of the Bear

Mrs. Mattson is meaner than Mrs. Schmidt. And the third grade is harder than the second grade. Mrs. Mattson not only hates my "sloppy" cursive writing, she also complains about the way I hold a pencil. "Mr. Rolo?" she says, standing in front of my desk, snatching my pencil from my hand. "You hold it this way." I try it her way until she turns her back to complain to another student, and then I slip the pencil back between my pointing and middle finger.

Mrs. Mattson also thinks I can't read as well as the other students. The first week of school, she sent a note home to my mother telling her I need to go to a special reading class twice a week for the rest of the year, maybe even next year as well. I'll be stuck with Mrs. Mattson for two years in a row. She teaches both the third and fourth grade classes, in the same room. I finally stopped thinking about looking forward to having Mrs. Baker for my teacher back at Lincoln Avenue Elementary in Milwaukee. My mother's Indian payment has not come, and my father is now making plans to cut enough wood to last through the winter, until spring and even the first part of next summer.

I think my mother has given up on getting that check from her tribe. She stopped asking me to walk to town to get the mail once school started again. I haven't heard her say anything to my father about going on a bus trip to Milwaukee to visit her sisters. And I haven't seen her writing any of her letters. She just keeps busy making her bread and reading her rummage-sale books that Irene gives her.

The only good thing about being back in school is not having to dig up row after row of potatoes and peel laundry baskets full of corn all day. But this morning, our father tells us to plan on coming straight home after school to help out with cutting wood. "And no one goes anywhere this weekend or the next," he says, rolling a cigarette. "We have to fill that basement up with as much wood as we can."

I am the first one off the bus after it squeals its brakes at our driveway. I zip up my jean jacket and watch all of the brown willow leaves swirling behind Whiskey as he races toward me. When we get close to the house, I see my father splitting birch wood. He yells at us to change out of our school clothes and "get right back out here!"

My mother is at the kitchen table, sewing cupboard curtains from an old white sheet with rose flower patterns. Just when I take off my jacket, she tells me to grab the big kettle and go downstairs to get a load of potatoes. I glare at her, wanting to ask her why we have to eat potatoes again. We've had mashed potatoes, fried potatoes, baked potatoes, and scalloped potatoes just about every night. But my mother glares back. "Don't get mouthy with me, or I'll make you peel 'em as well."

"But I'm supposed to change and go help the old man with the wood," I say.

"Good. You can do that right after you fill up that kettle for me," she says, looking back at her curtains.

I take my time picking the potatoes, putting them one by one in the kettle. I sit on the cement floor and watch my brothers toss chopped wood through the window. My father got a permit from the forestry department for that birch wood. He says we're going to burn a lot of it when it "gets down to forty below" this winter. But it's already getting colder. Some mornings when I wake up, I can see my breath.

When I get back upstairs, my mother is not in the kitchen. Philly is at the counter, mixing eggs and oatmeal in a bowl of hamburger. She tells me to start peeling potatoes.

"Where's Mom?" I ask as I place the kettle on the table.

"She doesn't feel well," Philly says. "Now, are you gonna peel those potatoes, or do I have to do that, too?"

I stand in the doorway of the bedroom and look at my mother. She is in bed, on her side. Robert climbs on top of her, laughing. I see a plastic ice cream bucket on the floor next to the head of the bed. She whispers to me to take Robert in the other room so she can rest. I gently sit on the edge of the bed and reach for my brother.

"Do you want me to read one of your Reader's Digest books to you?" I ask.

"Don't you have homework, a book to read?"

"No, we do all of that in the special reading class."

Robert squirms out of my arms and reaches for my mother's ankles. He puts his mouth on one of her snake scar burns and makes a sucking sound.

"What are you reading in class?" my mother asks.

I let out a big sigh and shake my head. "I don't know, some stupid book about a girl growing up in the woods with her dumb Ma and

Pa a hundred years ago. Do you want me to get your writing paper?
Do you wanna write to Aunt Sylvia or Frankie? Mom? How long
are you gonna need to rest?"

"Go see if I have any milk of magnesia left."

I carry Robert with me into the bathroom and open the cabinet
above the sink. But there's only my father's razor and shaving soap
on the shelves. I decide to ask my mother if she wants Philly to mix
her up some baking soda and vinegar. But when I stand in the doorway of the bedroom, her eyes are now closed. I put Robert down
on the floor and straighten out the covers, making sure they reach
down over her legs. Before I leave the room, I wait until I am sure
I can hear her soft breathing.

>[ ]<

When I finally race outside the school and start running home
before it gets too dark, I think about making up something to tell
my father when he asks me why I missed the bus. But telling him
the truth would only make things worse. I mouthed off to Mrs.
Mattson today when she looked at my spelling book, then slapped
it down on my desk and told me there is a *u* in the word *guess*.
I called her a liar.

But as soon as I reach the highway, I hear a car behind me. It's
my father's Oldsmobile. He pulls off to the side of the road. I hope
maybe he's been drinking at the bar and forgot about chopping and
piling wood today. I get in the backseat next to a big bag of chicken
feed. I glance at my father, seeing him holding the car lighter to his
rolled cigarette. His cap is on straight, and he's wearing his glasses.
He never wears his glasses when he drinks.

"What are you doing in town?" he asks.

"What do you mean?"

"You guys finish piling that wood like I told you?"

"Oh, yeah, I was helping, but Mom asked me to walk back into town to check the mail before the post office closed. So Dennis and the others, yeah, they finished piling up that wood."

"Your mother still in bed?"

Suddenly I spot a stack of letters on the dashboard.

"Yes, she forgot where you were today. That's why she wanted me to walk back into town."

My father looks in his side mirror, then turns back on the highway. He was in Littlefork all day, going to different farms, looking to find those Holsteins he wants to get before winter. He glances in the rearview mirror and says he was younger than me when he started milking cows. I tell my father that I would like to learn how to milk cows. I even tell him that maybe one day I might be running a farm when I'm older. He smiles at that, and I hope he remembers me telling him I'd like to be a farmer when my brothers squeal on me for not helping out with piling the wood.

"Your mother should feel a lot better when we get home," he says. "She got a letter from Frankie."

That's all my father can tell me about the letter from my oldest brother. My father wouldn't dare open any of my mother's letters. "It's the only damn privacy I got around this house," she says.

I think Frankie is her favorite. He goes to college in Milwaukee. Before we moved to Big Falls, he used to bring over his new girlfriend, Germaine. She wore a brown leather jacket and high-heeled boots. When the old man sat in the bar across the street, Frankie and Germaine would take our mother shopping, sometimes even to a movie show in his yellow convertible. The last Christmas Eve we had in Milwaukee, my father went to be bed early. He had no money for drinking. The only thing on the fake Christmas tree were strings of plastic icicles. Frankie and Germaine came by to visit our mother that Christmas Eve. Germaine picked out a bottle of perfume for her. The box had a big red bow wrapped around it. Every time I think about that night, about my mother smiling at Germaine, I think about that perfume. I wonder if my mother has it hidden somewhere in the house, waiting for the day when she can use it, waiting for the day when she can finally get to visit Milwaukee.

When we pull in the driveway, I see Scott and Philly standing on the porch, watching me. My father hands me the mail and says he has to unload the chicken feed.

"Boy, are you in trouble," Scott says to me. "Just wait until the old man finds out. He's gonna whip you with his belt."

"And Mom's gonna make you wash dishes all by yourself tonight," Philly says.

I hold up the stack of mail and tell them I don't think our mother is going to even care about me having to stay after school once she gets her letter from Frankie.

My mother sits up in bed when I tell her about the letter. We crowd around her, waiting for her to open it. But my mother takes her time reading the envelope. She finally shoves the unopened letter in her dress pocket and gets up. None of us ask why she won't open it now. We know she's going to save it for later. We know she likes to think about what's in the letter, sometimes more than actually reading it.

During supper, we watch our mother sitting on the couch with Robert. She's been reading and rereading Frankie's letter ever since we sat down at the table. Finally, as my father shakes more ketchup on his fried potatoes and hamburger, he asks our mother to "give us the news from Milwaukee."

Philly and I hurry up eating, then race into the living room. My mother hands over Robert to Philly, and she turns to the first page. She smiles and says, "Frankie is seriously thinking of proposing to

Germaine." She turns the page over. "He's hoping to graduate from
that Milwaukee technical college in the spring. He says I should wait
and come down next fall for the wedding."

"Well, those hens are really starting to lay now," my father says
to my mother. "Think of how much you can save in a year selling all
those eggs. What about your sisters? Frankie write anything about
Sylvia and Victoria?"

My mother only smiles again, then folds the letter, sticking it
back in her dress pocket. She reaches for Robert, holding him up
and kissing his fat cheeks until he starts to laugh.

My mother is still smiling when I see her the next morning. She
sits at the kitchen table with her writing paper and pen. My father
has his chainsaw torn apart, spread out on the dining room table. He
wipes his hands on an oily rag and says he has to drive into town and
see Merle Mac. "He's got some used parts in his shed I can buy."

"Can't you wait and mail this when I'm done?" my mother says.

"Corrine, it's Saturday. The post office closes at noon. You won't
have that letter written by then."

But my mother tells my father that even if it's the end of the day,
she wants to stop by the post office and drop off her letter so that it
can get mailed early Monday morning.

"I got a trailer of logs out there that need cutting and splitting,"
my father says. "I don't have the gas money to be making two trips
into town."

"Oh, for Pete's sake, Don! Go on, then. I'll just walk to the post
office."

My father takes off his glasses and rubs his eyes. He stands and
stares out the big picture window, past the smaller pine trees into
the gray, wet fields. "It's supposed to snow this afternoon," he says.

And then he takes out his tobacco pouch from his shirt pocket, still staring out the window. "Go ahead; finish your letter. I can work on the furnace. That damper still isn't working right."

I fill up a small pan with water and turn on the stove. I ask my mother if she wants any oatmeal, but she does not hear me because she's caught up in her writing. My father comes to the stove and bends his face down to the burner, lighting his cigarette.

"Frankie says your brother Tom called," my mother says to my father. "Your mother says she hasn't heard from you since we moved up here. I've been writing her here and there, but I guess she wants to hear from you."

My father tells me to hand him the box of oatmeal. He pours and stirs at the same time. I watch him turn down the flame. He hands me the spoon. "Just stir it until it gets real thick."

I lean against the counter, eating my oatmeal and watching my father sitting at the table with a piece of paper my mother gave him. He has his carpenter's pencil between his fingers. He looks at my mother. "Corrine? How does that Norwegian joke go? The one Hank told?"

"Your mother does not want to read that from you."

"How does it go?" he says. "Two pregnant women meet on the street—a full-blooded Norwegian and Chippewa. The Indian woman says . . ."

"No, that's not how it goes," my mother says, interrupting him. "The Norwegian woman brags she is carrying a full-blooded Norwegian baby. And the Indian woman smiles and says, 'I got a little Norwegian in me, too.'"

My father bursts out laughing. He keeps laughing until finally my mother does the same.

When my father finishes writing on a second page, he gets up from the table and stretches his arms over his head. My mother is still writing.

"When do you think you'll get those Holsteins?" she says to my father. "Frankie wants to know how the farm's coming along. He says he'd like to see it. He's thinking if his car is still running good, he might drive up here next summer."

"Sure, I could use the help. Milking a cow is like riding a bike. Frankie should still remember."

"He was thinking maybe you'd like to come to the wedding, too."

My father shrugs, then grins. "Ah, who's gonna watch the papooses if I go with you?"

>[ ]<

The snows hold off as we drive into town. The rainy, gray skies are turning darker. My father clicks on his headlights. My mother sits in the front seat with him, holding their letters. Dennis counts the last of his summer job money. He fixed the transistor radio, but it died again when Scott threw it at me, missing me and smashing it to pieces against the bedroom wall.

"Thirty bucks," Dennis says, slipping his wallet in his back pocket. Then he turns to me, whispering. "Think I should start carrying the new radio with me all the time? To school, the barn, even when I go cut wood with the old man? Where do you think would be a good place to hide it from you and Scott?"

I count the number of raindrops dripping down the window and think about the day I can get a summer job. I could buy my own school clothes, styles that I want and not those cheap blue tennis shoes our father buys us at the hardware store. I could buy my own stereo, start ordering record albums in the mail like Dennis. And maybe when Dennis graduates from high school and moves out, I can get one of the upstairs bedrooms all to myself, even if it has no wood heat.

My mother hands me the letters through the rolled-down window. She watches me as I slip the letters inside my jean jacket, then run to the mailbox slot at the post office. Dennis and my father go into the hardware store. When I get back to the Oldsmobile, my mother buttons up her black wool coat and tells me she'd better go into the Red Owl and get some of her hair dye.

Mrs. Mattson is standing at the counter when we walk in. She clips her purse shut, then ties her scarf under her chin. My mother smiles at her, and I avoid my teacher's eyes.

"I hear you're selling fresh eggs," Mrs. Mattson says to my mother. Then she looks at me, waiting until I look back at her. "Maybe you can bring me a dozen to school Monday morning."

I nod and stand closer to my mother, wanting to push her along. But my mother keeps smiling at Mrs. Mattson and asks her how I am doing, if I am behaving myself in class.

"He's a good guy," Mrs. Mattson says, reaching for her grocery bag. "His reading teacher says he's making very good progress. I'm thinking of asking him to read out loud in class."

Mrs. Mattson smiles at me and moves to the door. "Don't forget those eggs," she says. "And I'll see you at Mass tomorrow."

My mother checks out the prices of her hair dye and says she didn't know my teacher was Catholic. I tell her Mrs. Mattson comes to church alone. Her husband stays at home.

"You gonna come to church with us tomorrow?" I ask. "Maybe you could sit with Mrs. Mattson."

Merle Mac lives just across the river, up a hilly driveway into some thick pines. He has a station wagon that is almost as big as his one-room trailer house. Tractor engines and tires are scattered between the trees. He has three tin sheds with padlocks on them. We wait in my father's Oldsmobile and watch him carrying his chainsaw to the trailer. Merle Mac steps onto the porch steps. His little fuzzy brown dog sticks his head out the door and barks at my father. Merle Mac tosses a cigarette into the rain and grips his overhauls by the shoulder straps.

My mother flips on the dome light and reads the back of her hair dye box. Dennis sticks batteries in his new transistor radio and tries to find a station—nothing but static from the storm. He turns it off and leans over the front seat. "Hey, Mom? You getting excited about going to Frankie's wedding next year?"

"I gotta lose some of this weight and get my hair permed," she says.

"Gotta look your best, Mom," Dennis says. "Pretty as a white woman, right?"

My mother and Dennis laugh. I roll down my window and look across Merle Mac's driveway to the neighbor's yard. A black bear hangs by its neck from a tree branch.

"Look at that," I say. Dennis scoots over to my side of the Oldsmobile, and my mother rolls down her window. The bear swings in the freezing wind.

I look at my mother, wondering when she's going to roll up her window and tell my brother to tell the old man to hurry it up. But she does not roll up her window. She keeps her eyes glued to the dead bear. A white hunter comes out of his house with a long blade. The hunter goes to the bear and reaches up, stabbing the blade into the bear's neck. The hunter puts both hands on the blade's handle and starts cutting a line right down the center of the bear, all the way down to its hind legs. Black blood gushes everywhere.

I put my hands on my face, covering my eyes. I slowly open my fingers and look to see if my mother is doing the same. Her eyes do not even blink as she continues to stare at the hunter ripping into the dead bear.

"Can we go now?" I say to Dennis. "Can you go tell the old man to hurry it up? I want to go home. Please?"

>[ ]<

The farmhouse smells like wood smoke. Scott and I sit on the edges of the iron grate on the floor between the dining and living rooms with our bath towels, feeling the heat rise up on our feet and hands. We can hear our father beneath us in the basement, shoving in more wood, slamming the furnace door shut.

"Did you get up close to that bear?" Scott asks.

"Why?"

"Well, it was dead, right? Shoulda went up to it and seen how big his teeth were."

"Mom would have told me to stay in the car."

"No, she wouldn't. It was dead, right? The bear was already dead."

My mother is sitting at the kitchen table, writing another long letter. She has said nothing since we saw that bear. The supper dishes are still on the table. Dennis and the others are upstairs, trying to tune in a station on his transistor radio. Philly is in my mother's bedroom, reading her catechism book.

I hear my father's voice coming from the kitchen. "It's here—the first snow of the year."

I listen for my mother to say something.

"I don't know how much we're gonna get," my father says. "The older boys and I will have to saw up the rest of those logs all day tomorrow. I'll drive you and Philly to church."

Finally my mother speaks. "I'm not going to Mass in the morning."

I stand up and move closer to the kitchen, then sit at the dining room table where I can see my mother and father.

"Philly's got her First Communion coming up in a few months," my father says. "She can't be missing church. Hell, she should have made her First Communion three years ago like everyone else her age."

"Yes, and she'll have to wait another year," my mother says. "That priest lives in Northome. He's got three other churches to attend to."

"How in the hell would you know? You're never at Mass."

Suddenly my mother slams her pen on the table. "I'm not going to that goddamned church, and I'm not going back into that goddamned town! I'm going back to Milwaukee!"

"What the hell's gotten into you?" my father asks.

My mother gets up from her chair and moves to the stove. My father slowly reaches for the broom leaning against the wall. "Go ahead and take that damn thing," my mother says. "Hide it, burn it, do whatever you want with it." She reaches for a box of stick matches on the shelf above the stove and throws them at my father. "Take these, too. I don't want them. I told you. I'm going back to Milwaukee!" She fills the coffeepot with water and puts it back on the burner. My father stares at my mother. She stands by the stove with her arms folded, waiting for the water to boil.

My mother speaks again, softly this time. "You get your check next week, Don. I'm taking Philly and the baby."

I look up at my mother. "Once I sell another four or five days' worth of eggs, I'll have enough for gas money to pay Irene Cloutier. She and Hank can drive me to the bus station in Bemidji."

Whiskey gets up from the floor, stretches, then moves to stare out the picture window. The snows are thicker now, large flakes dripping down the window glass.

"These boys are old enough to take care of themselves around here, Don."

I look back at my mother, her eyes catching mine. "What the hell are you sitting there for?" she says. "Take the dog out so he can take a piss, for Christ's sake."

My father takes off his cap and looks at the floor.

I don't move my eyes from my mother.

"And don't you even think about getting mouthy with me," my mother says. "As far as I'm concerned, the next time you smart off to that teacher, she should just smack you upside the head." She quickly switches off the burner, then points her sharp finger at me. "Now, take that damn dog out like I told you!"

Whiskey follows me through the night snow. I stop long enough to dare myself to stare into the pines, sure that there is no longer any reason for me to be scared, sure because I know there's no more glowing bear. And I am right. It's dead.

I tell the dog to wait outside before I slip into the chicken coop. The yard light does not stretch far enough to light the inside. But I know my way. I hear the soft clucking of the hens and roosters sitting on their perches as I make my way to the back wall. My mother forgot to collect the eggs because she was so caught up in her writing all day. I reach inside the dark boxes and feel around the beds of hay. I grab six eggs in my arms and slip back outside.

I aim the eggs at the side of the chicken coop and splatter each one. I go back for six more and fire them off against the tin coop like the others. I almost go back for more, but then I think I've destroyed enough eggs that my mother can't sell.

The only light on now is in the kitchen. I kick off my rubber boots on the rug by the porch door. My mother is sitting at the table again, alone, writing her letter. I sit in my father's chair across from her. She does not look at me. I try reading her letter upside down, but I don't know cursive writing that well yet.

"Who are you writing to?" I hear myself asking out loud.

She breathes in, then turns over her page—more writing. "You need to go to bed," she says.

"Are you writing to Frankie?"

"You're old enough to start helping out around here now. Your father can't be on you boys all the time to help out."

"Are you telling Frankie you're leaving, Mom?"

"Quit staring at me and go to bed now."

"Mom? Are you really leaving? You really gonna leave us here with the old man?"

She sighs and slows her pen down. I wait until she looks up at me. I look down and see part of her left ankle, her snake scar burns. "Do you want me to hand wash your nylons, Mom? If I lay 'em on the grate, they'll be dry by morning in time for church."

My mother's ankle shifts. She rises and moves to the cupboards. She pulls back the rose curtains and slides out the box of Oxydol. She reaches for her bread mixing bowl. She fills the bowl with water and stirs in a handful of the laundry soap.

I go to her bedroom closet and grab a small laundry basket half full of my mother's things. When I return, the letter is gone from the table. I see her holding a paper bag of garbage. I reach out and trade my mother the laundry basket for the bag.

The wood furnace is four times bigger than my mother's oven. I use a stick to open the hot door and watch the birch sparking, listen to it crackling. I open the bag and find my mother's folded letter. There are five pages. I don't read a word of her writing. I look into the furnace flames for as long as it takes, stare until I see those glowing eyes again. And then I take each page of my mother's letter and feed them to the dying bear.

≫[9]≪

When the Land Whispers

The split second the football crashes into the Christmas tree, my mother goes for her broom. I don't duck behind the couch or run toward the bedroom. It wasn't my fault. John, he was the one who threw it too high for Joseph to catch. I was just sitting at the dining room table, pouring corn syrup on my pancakes.

"I don't know how many times I told you guys to quit throwing that ball in the house," my mother says, looking right into John's face.

But she never whacks at the brothers with her broom. Instead she begins sweeping up dead pine needles and a thousand pieces of all the glass ornaments that we or the cats have knocked down since the day we put up the tree. "God, I'll be glad when school starts again on Monday," she says.

I quickly eat as many of my pancakes as I can because I know she is going to start in on us, ordering us to clean up the house and to get our dirty laundry together. "Get dressed and haul this tree outside," she says to John.

"But it's thirty below," he replies.

"Then you better find a hat and gloves."

I don't care if it's thirty or a hundred below. I jump at the chance to drag the tree out all by myself. I know that once I get outside,

I won't have to do any cleaning or laundry. I can hide in the barn and put my hands and face against the warm sides of one of my father's new Holstein cows. Or I can build a fort with hay bales. I know I could last all day without freezing to death if I had to.

When my mother finishes sweeping, I hurry in and get my boots and coat on. I almost run to Philly's coat hanging on the wall. I steal the blue mittens from her pockets and stick them in my own. When John begins unscrewing the red and green iron tree stand, my mother tells Joseph to head out to the barn and help my father and Dennis. Joseph tries to get out of work by complaining that he doesn't want to get manure on his only good pair of jeans. I wait for my mother to threaten him with her broom. But she only shakes her head and goes to the kitchen. Joseph glares at me and tries to get me to go upstairs and find him some gloves. "Come on!" he orders. "You wore 'em last!"

I don't even look at him. I zip up my coat. Then I grab the tree with both of my bare hands. I leave a trail of pine needles and silver icicle strips as I pull the tree across the wood floor. In the kitchen, my mother sits at the table, peeling potatoes. "Don't leave that thing at the bottom of the steps," she says. "Drag it behind the garage."

Once I get the tip of the tree through the back door, I hear my mother's orders for everyone left inside: "Alright! Two of you! In the kitchen now! Dishes! The rest of you! Start picking up that living room!"

Just when I hear Philly start screaming at me to make sure I come right back inside when I'm done, I slam the door shut.

Suddenly I realize that the bright sun is just as freezing as the wind whipping against my cheeks. By the time I slip on my sister's mittens, my fingers are already numb. I push the tree down the porch steps. I grab it again with both hands. But even before I get a good grip, I realize the path to the garage is gone. The screaming winds have turned the farm into miles of white, rocky snowdrifts. Even the deep footprints leading to the barn are almost blown over. I think about leaving the tree where it is. But I can't go back inside. I just can't even think about scrubbing pots and pans. Not after all the work I did to get this damn tree out here!

I look up at the kitchen window and see Philly trying to find me. I lean up against the house and stare at the tree for a few seconds. I look back at the window, and when I don't see Philly, I move to the Christmas tree. I lift up the end of it and tumble it through the snow until I reach the corner of the house. I turn over the tree one more time. I climb on it, pushing it down, trying to bury it. Then I cover it up with as much snow as I can. Finally I take a break. I pull off my mittens and blow on my fingertips. I almost decide to head back inside and hope that most of the dishes are done. But then I hear my mother yelling that the "dishes have soaked long enough! Two of you kids better get in here before the water gets cold!"

The back door slams shut, followed by footsteps banging down the porch steps. I peek around the corner and see Joseph heading to the barn, pushing his way through the snowdrifts, mumbling, complaining. I look at the garage and think I could probably make it that far. I slip my mittens back on and think about how warm it might be inside my father's Oldsmobile.

Once Joseph disappears in the snow, I trudge my way to the garage. I sit in the backseat of my father's Oldsmobile and carefully, slowly close the door. I wrap myself up with a brown blanket and stare at the cold sun shining through the garage door window. I try remembering the last time I was here, maybe once or twice since we moved into the big farmhouse. My father tore down the bedroom walls and built a new sliding door so he and my older brothers could push his Oldsmobile inside. It stopped running around Thanksgiving, right after the four Holstein cows were delivered to the farm in a big cage trailer.

"Definitely need a new transmission," my father told my mother as she filled up an old coffee can with chicken feed in the garage. "When do you think that land payment check from the tribe will be coming?" She said nothing as she moved to the door with the bucket. He followed her. "How do you expect to get to town and back in this weather?" he yelled. "How we gonna haul groceries and that chicken feed?"

I stood in the garage doorway and watched my mother sprinkle the feed on the ground covered in new snow, calling the chickens. My father stood next to her with his hands on hips, waiting.

"You should never have bought those cows, Don," she said. "You knew that car was going out. You knew it was breaking down the day we moved up here."

"Are you gonna call up Odanah and find out about that check? Irene said you could use their phone anytime you needed, right? Didn't she say that?"

Suddenly my mother stopped feeding her chickens. She looked up at the dark gray clouds. I could see her hair flipping in the wind.

"Corrine?" my father yelled.

But my mother never looked at him. She lowered her head and stared across the white fields. "Don," she said as she moved her eyes to the row of white pine trees swaying in the wind, "I just don't think I'll get that payment."

"What did you say?"

There was a longer silence. And then my mother started back to the garage with the empty coffee can. I got out of her way, stepping outside. I didn't want to see my mother's eyes, so I stared across the fields like she did, feeling the wind swirling in my ears. "It means it might not come for a long, long time," she whispered. "Maybe years."

I listen to the stinging winter wind whipping through the cracks of the garage walls and pull the brown blanket as tight as I can around my legs and arms. I realize that I haven't heard my mother and father talk about that Indian payment—not once since Thanksgiving or anytime during the entire Christmas school break. I can't even think of a time when they argued since that morning. Even when the old man came home drunk, he never screamed at my mother. He was nicer to her more than ever before. Dennis said he was just trying to get on her good side in order to get his hands on her check. Sometime before Christmas, my father paid Merle Mac to drive my mother and him up to International Falls to buy a turkey, some oranges, walnuts, and bags of rock candy. The candy was all we had for presents on Christmas morning, but no one said anything bad about that, not even Dennis. I thought he would. I thought Dennis would laugh and tell my mother that it looked like Santa was pretty broke this year. That's what he would have said, but he didn't.

I can't feel my toes, so I decide I'd better get out of my father's Oldsmobile and walk around to try and warm up. I spot one of my mother's eyebrow pencils left on the window ledge. I think about drawing a picture of Thor or the Vision on the wall, but my fingers are too stiff from the cold. Maybe I could write a little note, I think, something like, "Mark Anthony was here." But I know when my brothers see it, they'll start teasing me for writing out my full name.

So I only write the date on the wall: "Sunday, January 2, 1972."

I draw a few puffy clouds around those letters and start thinking about our first New Year's Eve in Big Falls. It was better than the last one I remember, the time Aunt Sylvia slipped on the ice and cut up her knee on the south side of Milwaukee. Here in Big Falls, there was no all-night drinking in the farmhouse. My father stayed home with us instead of going to the tavern. "That's because he doesn't get his veterans check until Monday," Dennis said. "*After* the holiday."

But I forgot about what Dennis said because that night my father called Philly, Scott, Michael, and me into the kitchen. He wanted us to help him make a New Year's treat he used to have when he was a boy. He told us to pop up a lot of popcorn, enough to fill the big roaster pan. As soon as we melted the lard for the last batch, he mixed up some corn syrup and molasses in a different pan. When it started boiling, when it was just about ready, my father sprinkled in some baking soda. He stirred it as fast as he could before the syrup bubbled up over the pan's edges. And then he dripped it over the popcorn and told Philly and me to mix it all up. My father told us to set the roaster in a snowbank. It took only a few minutes for the syrup popcorn to cool off and harden up in the below-zero night.

After my sister and brothers scraped the last of the popcorn from the sides and bottom of the roaster pan, I saw my father coming up from the basement, hiding a bottle of 7UP under his arm. I watched as he went into the living room, sat down next to my mother, and popped it open for her. My father and my mother sat on the couch together the rest of the night, watching a music program that my mother had been looking forward to seeing for over a week.

"Guy Lombardo," my mother said. "Can you believe it, Don? They're actually going to show Guy Lombardo on Canadian TV."

I watched my father sitting close to my mother, and I wondered if he was really being as nice as it looked.

I hear my father's voice outside the garage, and I immediately put my mother's eyebrow pencil back on the windowsill. I rush to the door and look out the window. I blink my eyes, trying to see through the glaring sun. My father is pushing through the snow on his way back up to the farmhouse. I realize he is going to see the Christmas tree I left by the corner of the house. And when he does, I know what he'll do. He'll shake his head and storm up the porch steps. Once he gets inside the house, he'll want to know why I didn't haul the dead tree out behind the garage like my mother told me to do. But when he does notice the tree, he stops in his tracks, takes a long drag of his rolled cigarette, then reaches for it. He pulls the tree up on its end and stands it up in the snow. He straightens some of the fake icicles, then heads inside the house.

>[ ]<

When I come downstairs for breakfast, I see my mother pulling my sister's hair into a ponytail. Philly is sitting at the table, trying to pour milk into her cereal bowl with her mittens on. She probably wore them to bed, I think to myself, so no one would take them.

"Philly!" my mother says. "You're going to spill that everywhere."

"I thought you said you were gonna get after him for stealing my mittens," Philly says.

I sit across from my sister and put the Cheerios box between us so I don't have to look at her. "Hey," she says, holding her mittens above the box. "See these holes on the tips? It's because of all your slobbering and chewing."

"Just shut up and pass me the milk pitcher, Philly," I say.

We haven't had powdered milk ever since my father got his cows. I still eat margarine, though, because I can't stand the taste of the butter. None of us eat the cow butter except my mother and father.

When Scott sits down, I turn the cereal box so I don't have to look at him, either. He pissed the bed last night. I kicked at him when I woke up to find the blanket soaked. We don't have many blankets, and since there is barely any heat upstairs, I had to put on my coat to keep warm.

"My coat smells like piss," I say to my mother as she threads a needle for Philly's mittens.

"Watch your mouth," my mother says.

"Well, I can't go to school smelling like pee."

"That was you," Scott says. "You peed last night."

I don't bother kicking my brother under the table because my mother knows I didn't piss the bed. She knows I haven't wet the bed in months.

"I'm wearing *your* coat, Scott," I say as I push my chair back and stand up.

"No, you're not," he says. "Mom?"

My mother breathes out, putting her needle and thread on the counter. She takes off her glasses and rubs her eyes. I look at the broom by the refrigerator. "Go downstairs and get a scoop of laundry detergent," she quietly says to me.

"I'm not scrubbing that coat!" I say.

"I'll do it!" my mother says. "God, I can't wait for that bus to get here."

In the basement, my brother Dennis is ironing his blue shirt. He stands in a puddle of melted snow from his boots. Dennis and Joseph had to get up early to help milk the cows and shovel a pathway to the road. "Why you doing that?" I ask.

"Because my shirt's wrinkled," he replies. "Is there another reason why a person irons that I don't know about?"

"You excited about going back to school, Dennis?"

He turns over his shirt and slides the iron along one of the sleeves. "Yeah, I'm excited. Beats sitting around this place, shoveling snow and cow shit all day."

"You're excited about seeing your girlfriend, right?"

Dennis smiles, then adjusts a knob on the iron.

"You haven't seen her since we got out for Christmas. I thought you were gonna hitchhike up to Littlefork to see her on New Year's."

"I was, but I decided it wasn't worth fighting with the old man. Farm chores, you know?" But then Dennis sets the iron on its end and stares at his blue shirt. He says he was too embarrassed to hitchhike to see Angie. He says he was hoping to get his driver's permit, but when the old man's Oldsmobile broke down, he just put her out of his mind.

"But that piece-of-shit car is not a problem anymore. I got me a free bus ride thanks to the Littlefork–Big Falls School District. I can see Angie five days a week."

Dennis hops up the basement steps with his shirt hanging over his shoulder, and I scoop up a cup of Oxydol. I never bothered asking him if he was still hoping we would move back to Milwaukee. I guess I could tell by the way he smiled about his girlfriend that he was forgetting about the south side, forgetting about our Indian cousins and his old friends like Harry Petree. Harry is the one who taught Dennis how to smoke cigarettes and maybe even how to iron a shirt.

Even I was eager to get back to school. The last time I saw my friends, the twins Rick and Robbie, was the day before Christmas break when Mrs. Mattson let us have a party in the afternoon. She made everyone in class a brown bag of candy canes, a brownie, and peanuts. I was excited about seeing Mike Hovan, too. I figured he would probably be wearing new Dingo boots or expensive jeans he got for Christmas. That was the only part about going back to school that I wasn't looking forward to: having to make up presents I never got when it was my turn to tell everyone in class.

When I get back upstairs, my mother is already scrubbing my coat with some soap she had underneath the sink. "What are you gonna do today, Mom?" I ask.

"Well, I have a lot of things to do after cleaning. I want to finish that book Irene gave me." She points to a plastic bag on top of the refrigerator. "And after Robert goes down for his nap, I need to finish making Philly's dress for her First Communion."

"What about the old man's disability check? Doesn't he get paid today? Think he's gonna sit at the bar all day?"

"Put this on," she says, handing me my coat. "The bus will be here any minute."

> *{ }*

We stand at the top of the driveway and watch the bus turn off the highway and make its way down the snow-covered dirt road. I can keep only one hand in my coat pocket because I have to hold my tablet and math workbook with the other. My sister looks at my red fingers. She slips off her mittens and holds them out to me. "You can wear them just for today if you promise not to chew and slobber on them," she says. "And when you get home tonight, you better look for your pair."

When I hear the squeal of the bus brakes and big tires crunching against the snow, I glance back at the farmhouse and see the smoke rising out of the chimney into the blue sky. I think about something my father said before Dennis yelled that the bus was coming. My father was pouring my mother the last cup of coffee. He asked her to sit with him at the table. My father told her he decided he was going to wait on walking to town to pick up his veterans check. "It's supposed to stay below zero all day. But it'll be warmer tomorrow."

I don't know why my father isn't anxious to get his check and go to the bar this morning. I know he has bills to pay, bills that he talks about at night, like fixing his Oldsmobile. I wonder if maybe Dennis was right—maybe he's just being nice because he wants my mother's Indian payment. Before I get on the bus, I look back one more time at the farmhouse and wish my father would walk to town this morning. I wish he would go to the bar like he's always done in the past.

A Cat's Storm

Tabby has been gone for the past three days now. She left her sleeping kittens in the birch woodpile, came up the basement steps, and scratched and cried at the back door until someone let her out. She leaped across icy puddles and disappeared in the brown field behind the barn. But it snowed that night. It snowed through the next morning. When the storm left, we waited for Tabby to come home to her kittens. But even though the snow melted almost as fast as it fell, that cat never returned.

The six kittens are old enough to drink milk and eat the bits of raw hamburger that Philly and I give them. Yesterday, Philly told us we should move them from the woodpile and hide them in the upstairs attic. "We'll have to take turns feeding them," she said. "And we have to make sure the door is shut at all times."

But the kittens miss their mother. Their crying is louder. This afternoon, my father yells at us to bring them downstairs. And when we do, each of us carrying two kittens in our arms, we see a cardboard box on the kitchen floor. My father says when he was at the Littlefork feed store, he got to talking to a farmer who was looking for some good mousers.

Philly kisses and then puts the last kitten, Brownie, in the box. I steal a piece of my mother's meat loaf mix from the bowl while she digs for a bread pan in the cupboard. Whiskey sniffs around the box, then licks my greasy hand when I push him away. Before Philly folds down the last lid of the box, my brother Michael kneels down on the floor and reaches for Brownie. He holds the kitten up and asks if we can keep at least one.

"We got too many cats around here," my father says, lighting his cigarette. "I wouldn't mind so much if you kids would have just left those kittens in the barn where they belong. Why do you think that mother kept moving them from place to place? To keep them away from you kids. She was an outdoor cat. And that's where she wanted her kittens to be."

When my father takes the box, placing it under his arm, Whiskey jumps up and leans against his hip, sniffing at the box again. Michael quickly starts putting on his rubber boots. "I wanna go with you, Dad," he says. "I can sit in the backseat with the kittens to keep them from escaping from the box."

But my father says he has to go, that Merle Mac is wasting gas in the driveway. My mother doesn't wait for my brother to start bawling. She wags her finger at Michael and tells him if he's going to make a big deal about having to stay home, he can just take it in the other room. Then she moves back to the table and cracks another egg in a bowl, calling me to come and finish making the meat loaf. "Wash your hands first."

"What if Tabby comes home?" Philly asks.

I wait for my mother to answer her, but she doesn't. Instead she reaches on top of the refrigerator for a plastic bag—Philly's First Communion dress.

Philly's voice gets louder. "How do you think she's going to feel when she finds out her babies are gone?"

My mother slips the white dress out of the bag, unfolding shiny, smooth sleeves. "I wish I had the material to make you a veil, Philly," she says. "But Irene says she has a rhinestone tiara that her daughter wore when she made her First Communion."

"You shouldn't have let him take those kittens, Mom!" Philly yells. "Why did you let the old man take them?!"

My mother turns with the dress and holds it out for Philly to see. "Listen," she softly says. "That cat is not coming back."

"You don't know that, Mom!" Philly yells.

"Forget about that cat," my mother says, sighing.

"Why? Did the old man give Tabby away, too? Is that what happened to her? Why did you let him take her away from her babies?"

Suddenly my mother reaches for the bread pan and slams it on the table. "Philly! No one did anything to that cat! She knew exactly what she was doing! She *knew* that snowstorm was coming!"

I close my eyes and wish my sister would just stop going on about Tabby. When I open my eyes again, Philly is sniffling as she stares at the floor.

My mother's voice gets soft again. "Forget about the cat and think about your First Communion." She turns with the dress. "Now, come with me and try this on. We only have a few days left to make sure it fits."

But Philly doesn't stop like I hope. She grabs the bread pan and whips it across the room, almost hitting Whiskey. The dog hides his tail between his legs and scoots under the table. My mother looks back just as Philly runs by her, screaming, "I'm not trying on anything! I don't want to be a part of this family anymore!"

My mother quietly tells me to pick up the pan and wash it. I do like she says. I set the clean bread pan back on the table and watch her folding up Philly's dress, putting it on top of the refrigerator.

"Did you rinse that pan?" she asks.

"Yes."

"Then get the meat in it."

"But I don't know how to make meat loaf."

She moves toward me and speaks every word slowly and clearly like she does when she thinks none of us are listening closely, when she thinks we're trying to secretly get out of doing work. "Put the meat in the pan. Put the pan in the oven. Close the oven door."

As soon as I do like she says, Philly comes back into the kitchen with a brown paper bag. She is wearing the green velvet spring jacket that my mother found for her at a rummage sale last fall. Philly has been anxious to wear that jacket once it gets warmer out.

"Where do you think you're going?" my mother says.

Philly wipes her eyes with the backs of her hands and sits at the table. "I'm leaving." And then she looks at me. "You're coming with me, right?"

"What?" I say as I dry my hands on a dish towel. "I can't go anywhere. I have to watch the meat loaf."

My mother reaches for a small pan on the stove and asks me to fill it up with water. She lights a top burner and reaches for a tea bag and chipped white cup. "It's supposed to snow again, Philly," she says.

"I know that!"

"Well, you sure you're gonna be warm enough in that jacket?" my mother asks.

But Philly ignores her, knowing she is only trying to talk her out of going. This is not the first time Philly's decided to run away from home. Last summer, she stayed away a whole week at her friend Jackie Gertz's house. I forget about how our fight started, but she must have been angrier than I knew at the time. I had a bump on my forehead for days because she whacked me with a shoe.

"Why are you standing there looking at me?" she says. "Get your coat. We're leaving now!"

My mother turns to me and shrugs. "Get your coat on. I don't want her out in the cold by herself."

"What do you mean by that, Mom?" Philly says, zipping up her jacket.

"Go before it gets dark, Philly. But you better be back here by Sunday morning. There's gonna be hell to pay if you don't."

>[ ]<

Philly says we have to take a different route to get to Jackie's house. And she doesn't want to take the train tracks because our father could still spot us from the highway when he comes back. I follow her toward the barn. John once told us that it was actually a shorter path to town if we walked through the back field.

But even though most of the snow is melted around the yard, it's deeper than it looks in the fields. Philly and I make it only as far as a patch of small willow trees. My sister didn't give me enough time to find my boots, so I had to wear my tennis shoes. I lean against one of the willow trees and tell Philly that maybe we should wait until tomorrow or maybe a few more days until more snow melts.

"We're not going back," she says, reaching in her brown paper bag. "Here, Mom made some cheese sandwiches for us. I think if we walk along the power lines, there will be less snow. Hurry up and eat."

I take my time with the sandwich and stare at some tiny animal tracks in the snow. Probably from a mouse, I think. "Philly? Do you think Tabby is out here? Maybe she's busy hunting, trying to get fatter so she has enough milk for the kittens. John says that's why she left. She went on a long hunting trip because she needed more milk."

Philly snaps some willow twigs, then looks up at the sky. Snowflakes are falling. It's also getting darker sooner than we thought it would. I tell her there's no way we can make it to town. We'll get lost in the snowstorm, be stuck out here, and freeze.

"Well, we're just going to have to make a fire," she says, snapping a twig in her hand. "There are a lot of branches we can use."

I don't bother reminding my sister that we have no matches. I look at the shadows of the willows on her face, and I am scared. She leans against the tree next to me and closes her eyes. I hope she's forgetting about being as mad as she was in the house. I hope she's thinking about turning back.

"What about your First Communion on Sunday?" I ask. "Ain't you curious about what those little round white things taste like? John says it doesn't even taste like real bread."

"It's not supposed to. It's the body of Christ."

"I don't know what that means," I say. "I don't know what anything in church means."

Philly whispers that she'd like a sandwich. I nod and quickly hand her one. She closes her eyes again, then takes a small bite.

"Tabby's not coming home," she whispers. "She's never coming back."

I take the last bite of my sandwich, then wait with Philly. The snow falls into the forest now, finding us. My sister opens her eyes and leaves the rest of her sandwich on the ground. She stands and holds her bag of clothes in her arms.

"Why are you leaving your sandwich?" I ask.

"For Tabby," she says, shrugging. "Just in case."

Suddenly the snow feels warmer, like a blanket floating down on us. I pull off my cap and gloves and walk with Philly out of the willow forest and into the field. The lights of the farmhouse glow like kerosene lamps—burning all night—however long it takes for Philly and me to reach home again.

$\gg[\,1\,1\,]\ll$

The Last Bloom of Lilacs

My father is alone in the barn. Early this morning, he stood at the open door and watched men haul away his Holstein cows in their cage trailer. And then he went back inside, probably to reread the letter telling him that if he missed another month's payment, they would have to come and take back their cows.

I look away from the window above the sink and finish washing the fresh eggs. I carefully dry each one, then place them in the used cartons for my mother to sell. Michael sits at the table, trying to open my father's can of Prince Albert tobacco. He wants to roll a cigarette and bring it to the barn. I tell him it takes years to learn how to roll a cigarette. "You're gonna spill tobacco everywhere, and then I'm the one who's gonna get blamed for it." But he doesn't listen. He pulls at the lid with his chubby fingers, even bangs the can on the table. Finally he opens a counter drawer and digs through spoons and forks. "Hey! Don't touch that knife," I say, slamming the drawer shut. I pick up the can and papers. "Here, just take it to him."

I wouldn't think of bringing my father his tobacco unless he asked me to. He likes Michael more than the rest of us. My father sometimes lets Michael sleep with him in his bed, especially when

Michael comes downstairs in the middle of the night, crying from a nightmare he had. Michael follows through the garden rows and even to the edge of the fields with my father. When my father realized the problem with the Oldsmobile was worse than a bad transmission, he had to make the decision to buy a used motor for the car instead of making payments on the Holsteins. Michael wanted to help him put in the motor. He spent a whole weekend in the garage holding tools for my father.

When I put the last egg carton in the refrigerator, I realize I'd better head outside and protect Michael from the rooster. Even I get attacked by that rooster when I'm not looking. He doesn't like any of us. He raises his wings and charges at us for no reason, picking at our legs with his sharp beak and jumping at us with his claws. But I got lucky when I was collecting eggs earlier this morning. That rooster did not see me slip into the chicken coop to get my mother's eggs because he was busy picking and scratching at something, maybe an anthill, on the side of the road.

The rooster is still on the road, but Michael runs as fast as he can toward the barn, holding his baggy pants. I drop the rock I picked up from the driveway and wait until my brother gets to the barn. My father meets Michael at the open door, smiling, taking the tobacco from him.

I head back to the house and see my mother still hanging bedsheets on the clothesline. I reach the porch, then hear her call my name. Right away I want to start asking why I am the only one around here who has to work. "Why can't I go to town like everyone else?"

"Did you wash all of those eggs?" she asks.

"Yes. Can I go with you when you go to town to sell 'em?"

She hangs the last sheet on the line and pulls her hair away from her face. "Get me some clothespins," she says.

I reach in the basket and grab a handful. "Well? Can I go with you?"

"I'm not going to town. Not today."

"Why?"

She looks over her shoulder toward the barn. My father and Michael are coming up the path. "How many cartons are there?" my mother asks.

"I don't know, maybe six. How come you're not going to town?"

"Listen, you get inside and take five of those cartons to the basement and hide them under the stairs."

I look back at my father, and I know what she means. The old man is broke. Because he had to buy that used motor, he didn't have much left over from his check for drinking. Two six-packs of Pabst was all he brought home after spending the rest on groceries and the electric bill.

When I get back up the basement steps, I look out the back door. My father is helping my mother hang the last sheet. I watch until she shakes her head no, then I duck and step into the kitchen.

"What's going on?" John asks, pouring sugar in a warm jar of instant coffee.

"It's the old man," I say, peeking out the window. "He wants to get drunk. He wants to sell Mom's eggs."

"Let's go upstairs," he says. "I don't wanna listen to him raising hell with Mom."

I don't go upstairs with John. I know sooner or later the old man is going to come looking for me. He's going to ask me where I hid those eggs. I decide to sneak out through my mother's bedroom.

I remember she had the old man pry open her window because the room smelled with so much bleach from her mopping.

Once my bare feet hit the grass, I head to the front of the house and sit on the cracked cement steps. I breathe hard and stare at the old porch, a pile of broken cement and black wood beams. It used to be a beautiful porch, my father once said. It extended from one side to the other of the house. In the springtime, they used to replace the windows with screens so people could sit and enjoy the summer nights without getting bit up by mosquitoes. But when the fire came through here, the porch floor and roof collapsed. My father said it would cost a fortune to try and rebuild it. The only thing that survived the fire is some lilac bushes on each side of the steps.

I wait until I hear the back door closing. I crawl down the steps and slide underneath some of the lilac bushes. I get on my stomach and get close enough so I can see my father putting all of the egg cartons in the backseat of his Oldsmobile. Michael wants to get in, but my father takes him by the hand and points him to the house. When I hear the engine starting, when I see my father turning on the dirt road toward town, I roll over on my back and close my eyes.

I never really noticed the sweet smell of those lilacs until now. And I realize the flower bushes smell even sweeter once the sound of my father's Oldsmobile fades, once he gets farther and farther away from home.

>[ ]<

My mother tells Philly to go inside and wrap a fresh loaf of her bread in tinfoil. She won't take no for an answer when she offers Irene and Hank Cloutier her bread. Irene tries to hand her two cartons of eggs. The Cloutiers said the old man came by the house saying he needed the egg money to buy some quarts of oil for his Oldsmobile, that the used engine had a leak in it. But my mother tells her to keep the eggs. She insists.

As always, Hank gets out of the car to smoke his cigarette, and Irene stays in the front seat, holding and playing with my brother Robert. My brothers and I sit on the grass along the driveway, smiling. Irene likes to try and tickle us if we get too close to her. My mother leans against the Cloutiers' white car with her arms folded, close to her chest. She stares at the red sun falling in the cold spring evening.

"He had that glazed look in his eye, Irene," my mother says. "I knew he'd never take no for an answer. And I was just too damn tired to fight with him. So I said, 'Go ahead, Don. They're under the basement steps. Take those eggs. Get drunk off your ass.'"

"How can you get drunk on a few dozen eggs?" Irene says, laughing.

"Ah, he's a bullshitter," my mother says. "Don gets to talking to someone, then offers to buy him a drink, and before you know it, he's getting two free drinks for the one he bought."

Philly returns with the loaf of bread, and Irene says she must have a bite. She nods and tells my mother she should think about selling her bread and cinnamon rolls along with her eggs. But my mother only smiles and tells Irene that she doesn't think anyone would buy her bread. "Everyone knows how to bake bread."

"Hey, Irene," I say. "You want some lilacs?"

"You got lilacs?"

"Yeah, didn't you see 'em when you drove up?"

"Go get a bunch," my mother says.

"I love lilacs," Irene says. "We don't have a lilac bush." She winks at us and smiles. "I keep telling Hank to steal some from the Nelsons next door. They smell *so* pretty. But they don't bloom for long, I tell him. You have to get them now. But he never listens to me, so we go another year without."

I snap off the lilacs and tell Scott to hold out his arms. I grab some for my mother as well.

When we return to the driveway, my mother is rocking Robert in her arms. Irene buries her nose in the flowers and giggles. "They tickle," she says, catching me off guard, pinching my gut.

Hank takes one more drag of his cigarette and says they should be heading home. My mother hands over Robert to Philly. Irene's smile disappears, and she leans her head out the window, whispering to my mother. "You know about Moose Lake, Corrine? It's a place for people to dry out. It's located down toward the Cities. You could get Don committed, force him to sober up for good."

"I'll have to get a job to support these kids," my mother says. "Where am I gonna get a job in Big Falls?"

"No, you don't. Any judge in his right mind would be happy to order Don to sign over his veterans check every month to you. Why should you keep putting up with his shit? He's the one who has to change, not you. Not you, Corrine."

My mother is silent for a few seconds.

Irene says, "Thanks again for the eggs and lilacs."

"Let me get you another loaf of bread," my mother says.

"Too late," Irene says, smiling at us. "Hank is already backing up the car. Right, Hank?"

When we get inside the house, Philly fills a canning jar with water for the lilacs. She sets them on the oak dining table and asks my mother if she likes them.

My mother says she likes them very much as she pulls a chair up to the big picture window. She sits down and stares through it. "The old man's gonna be here soon," I say.

"I know," she says.

"Don't you want us to get your pillow and blanket? Maybe we could sleep in the barn."

"I'm not going anywhere. Now, you kids let me be. Go and eat some of that chili I made."

When we finish eating in the kitchen, we don't bother washing the dishes. I think about asking my mother if we can watch TV if we promise to turn it real low. But she looks back at us and tells all of us to go upstairs. Before we leave, she tells Philly to take Robert as well. "Go!" she says.

[ ]

Sometimes I wake up to a nightmare. Tonight it's my mother's scream. The nightmare opens my eyes to stare at a streak of black blood running along the ceiling. And then the claws of her scream reach up from the floor and tear into my arms and legs, pinning me down against the bed. I can't move a muscle.

"Get outta the way!" Joseph says, pushing me off the bed. I don't mind the pain of hitting the wood floor. I am relieved that I can now move.

I follow my older brothers through the dark to the top of the stairs. Light from the kitchen flares up the steps.

"You're no damned good!" my mother screams. Then glass smashing, something, the jar of lilacs shattering against the floor.

Dennis points at me to get back into bed. But I take only a few steps away, watching Joseph and him jump down the stairs.

But before they can reach her, the nightmare turns even darker. I hear the slap of his hand on her. I press my fingertips deep into my ears until I am deaf.

The nightmare ends only when I see my brother John coming slowly up the stairs. He doesn't look at me as he passes by, but he does speak. "Let's just say Dennis and Joseph hit him harder than he hit her."

I sit on the floor and put my head between my legs, hoping she will stop crying, hoping her tears will dry by the time daylight comes. It's the only way I can be sure that the worst of the nightmare is over.

>[ ]<

My mother won't come out of her bedroom. She's been in there since we woke up. Philly is in the kitchen, wrapping ice cubes in a towel. Scott is at the stove, pouring oatmeal in boiling water. Michael stands on a chair next to him, holding a bowl and spoon.

I sweep up glass and wet, dying lilacs. The top of the oak dining table is on the floor, broken off from the legs. John comes through the back door. "Well, it must be pretty bad," he says. "They've been gone for more than three hours."

He tells me to come and help him lift the tabletop back on its legs.

John says he watched the whole thing. "Dennis and Joseph jumped on the old man when they saw Mom on the floor. They knocked him down. The old man put his hand on the edge of the table to try and get up. But the tabletop was loose, and it came crashing down on his ankle. I bet he busted it in three places at least."

John holds the dustpan for me. Rain begins to fall against the picture window. I think about that stupid rhyme the old man says when he's in a good mood: *April showers bring May flowers.*

I ask my brother if he knows how long the old man might be in the hospital. He says maybe for a few days. "But I wouldn't get your hopes up for any time longer than that."

Philly comes in from my mother's bedroom. She looks at the dustpan of glass and lilacs and says we should take it straight out to the pit.

Whiskey knows where we throw and burn the garbage. He runs ahead of John and me to the back of the garage. When we reach the pit, Whiskey is busy sniffing empty tomato paste and kidney bean cans, macaroni boxes, and rags—old clothes too torn for my mother to save with her needle and thread. John takes out a book of matches and tries to light up some damp newspapers. Smoke rises and stings my eyes.

"Mom waited at the window until she saw his headlights, the old man turning off the highway onto the dirt road," John says. "It was nine minutes before midnight. I know because I was in the kitchen watching the clock."

"Mom let you stay downstairs with her?"

"I told her I wasn't going to let the old man raise hell with her."

I stand on the other side of my brother to avoid the smoke. "It's not gonna burn," I say. "It's too wet." But John strikes more matches. He even tries to burn what is left of the lilacs.

"She was going to give him an ultimatum," he says, not looking at me. "You know what that is?"

"I know what it means."

John strikes another match and stares into the smoke. "I watched him from the kitchen window. The dumbass left the headlights on, so I ran outside and stood around the side of the house. When he staggered inside, I went and turned off the headlights." John coughs from the smoke and wipes his burning eyes. "Wanna know why I did that? I wanted to make sure the battery wouldn't die. I wanted Dennis to drive the old man back to town and leave his drunken ass at the bar."

The light rain picks up. I wipe Whiskey's nose and ears, stroking his wet fur.

"I got between him and Mom, shoving back," he says. "But he kicked me in the thigh."

I tell John that I'm getting wet and cold.

"And then he went after Mom."

"I'm going back inside now," I say.

"Why? Don't you want to hear the rest?"

"No, I don't." I stick my fingers in my ears and yell for Whiskey to come. But as I step around my brother, he turns and grabs my shirtsleeve, holding me. "Knock it off, John. Let me go!"

"But I haven't told you the rest," he says, standing and gripping my arm tighter. "Don't you want to know what the old man did next?"

I twist away from him, slipping, falling in the mud. "That's it! I'm telling Mom right now what you just did!"

"What are you gonna tell her? That you didn't want to hear about how he slapped her, slammed her against the wall? You gonna tell her you didn't want to believe that she married a violent drunk? Is that what you're gonna tell her?"

"I know he's a drunk!" I yell.

"You don't have a clue! You have no idea!" John breathes hard and rubs his face. "Then go. Go ahead," he says, walking away from me. "Tell Mom. Tell her anything you want."

I quickly reach for a tomato paste can and throw it at him, missing by a mile. I sit up in the mud and stare at his wet newspaper ashes.

When I come around the side of the garage, I stop and stare at the window of my mother's bedroom, dripping in the rain. Suddenly my anger disappears. I decide I'm not going to tell my mother about

John knocking me down in the mud. I won't ask her to do anything. I won't quietly step into her bedroom and look away from her bloody eyes. I won't sit next to her and gently lean against her sore shoulder or softly kiss her purple skin. I won't ask if I can get her a glass of cold water and some aspirin. I won't ask her why she married a violent drunk. I decide I won't ask my mother anything.

≫[12]≪

Rocket Son

Whiskey is the first to spot my older brother James coming down the dirt road with a red duffel bag hanging over his shoulder. The dog barks nonstop as he races across the front lawn and jumps over the ditch. He stands guard in the middle of the road growling, his tail and the hair on his back straight up. But when James drops his bag, takes off his round wire-rimmed sunglasses, and calls out to him, the dog's bark turns to a high-pitched whine. Whiskey must remember the sound of James's voice. My brother was there the night Whiskey's mother gave birth to him in the foster home back in Milwaukee. A judge ordered James to live at the foster home because he was skipping high school and because he had more trouble trying to get along with the old man than any of the other brothers.

My mother bought a new box of hair dye. It's still on the windowsill in the dining room because she hasn't had any time to use it. She has been baking more bread and cinnamon rolls ever since she talked with James on the phone when he called long distance to Hank and Irene's home two days ago. The Cloutiers drove out to the farm to tell my mother she needed to get in the car and go with them because James would be calling back.

The old man did not even bother to come out of the house to say hi to Irene and Hank. I saw him with his crutches under his arms, peeking out of the kitchen window

Before my mother got in the backseat, she said everyone had to stay home. But Scott and I raced alongside Irene and Hank's car as far as we could down the dirt road. Just before Hank speeded up and left us in the dust, my mother smiled and yelled at me to sweep out one of the upstairs bedrooms so James would have a place to sleep once he got here.

By the time we get to the dirt road, James is on one knee, hugging Whiskey. He looks more like a hippie than the last time we saw him. James's black hair is longer, stretching past his shoulders. He wears bell-bottom jeans and a silver watch. Of course, he starts right in on teasing my brothers and me for having butch haircuts and dirty faces.

"What do you got in the bag?" I ask. "Did you bring us anything?"

"Maybe," he says, smiling. "Where's Philly?"

Scott and I carry James's duffel bag as we walk back to the house. I tell him Philly just left for camp. Mrs. Barthel, the Koochiching County social worker, said Philly could go to Camp Buckskin for free. "She's gonna be away for five weeks," I say. "Do you think you'll still be here by the time she gets back, James?"

My mother wears the best dress she has—dark blue with three white buttons and sleeves that reach past her elbows. When Scott and I drag James's duffel bag up the stairs and into the muggy kitchen, I see sweat dripping down the sides of her neck. Right away James puts his arms around her and squeezes. My mother doesn't like hugs. Dennis once told me that's an old Indian thing. A lot of Indians have a hard time making a big deal out of seeing someone they haven't seen in a very long time, especially if it's a son or daughter.

When the old man hobbles into the kitchen on his crutches, James looks at his ankle. They removed the cast over a week ago.

"Well, how's it going, James?" the old man says, putting out his hand.

"It's cool," James says.

"Sorry I couldn't meet you at the bus stop, but I can't drive too long before my ankle starts acting up."

"I caught a ride at a truck stop outside of Bemidji."

"Oh, yeah, those trucks are always up and down the highway. Say, you wouldn't happen to have an extra smoke on you, would you?" After James hands him one of his Kent cigarettes, he turns away. The old man runs his hand through his hair, then hobbles back to his bedroom.

James doesn't say anything until he hears the old man's door close. He looks around the kitchen and moves to the dining room. "Where's everyone else? Dennis? Joseph?" he asks.

My mother tells him the older guys are working their summer jobs. Dennis is mowing lawns for the city, and Joseph is scrubbing floors at the grade school. "You're gonna stay for awhile, right?" my mother asks.

James puts his hands in his back pockets and stares out the big picture window, smiling. "So, Mom, tell me all about Big Falls, Minnesota."

>[ ]<

Once we finish the hamburgers my mother fried up for dinner, James starts bossing us around like he did when we lived in Milwaukee. My mother laughs when he jokes about getting after us with the broom if "you papooses don't get and do those damn dishes like I tell you!"

Scott and I rush through the dishes so we don't miss out on what James and my mother are talking about as they sit together at the dining table, drinking coffee and eating cinnamon rolls. James says he stayed at the foster home until he graduated from high school a week ago. He says things are pretty much the same with Aunt Sylvia and the other sisters. "Still drinking, still arguing over who knows more about being Indian. That's why cousin Earl moved out of Milwaukee, Mom. He got sick and tired of getting calls at three in the morning from those sisters wanting him to settle arguments about the Chippewa language."

My mother asks about Jerry, who is a year older than James.

"Not doing much, just running with the Sawicki brothers," he says. "Jerry says he'd like to visit but thinks it's too far to hitchhike."

And she asks about Frankie. She tells James the last letter she got from Frankie was in April. He wrote about his proposing to Germaine. They haven't set a date yet.

"Who knows with Frankie?" James says as he reaches down to his duffel bag on the floor by his feet. "I slept on his couch for a few days, then he started getting on my ass about looking for work. I said, 'For Christ's sake, Frankie, I just graduated. Can I just enjoy the moment?'"

My mother says nothing after that. She just smiles and looks at James as he digs through his bag.

Then James says he's decided he's sick and tired of Milwaukee and all those "plastic hippies" hanging around on the lakefront. "You know where I'd like to live, Mom? Minneapolis. I had a four-hour layover in downtown Minneapolis. God, you should see that city. They just built a new skyscraper made of glass."

He pulls out some albums, ones he bought with the allowance he got every week while at the foster home. He tells us we can look at them but not to take them out of the cases. We spread them out on the table: Elton John, James Taylor, and Santana.

James reaches over and touches the edge of my mother's blue dress sleeve. "That's a beautiful dress, Mom, but you must be burning up in that thing," he says.

"I would get a part-time job, but there's no work for me in this town," she says. "The only work is the mill."

"The mill? What kind of mill?" James asks.

"They got a sawmill just across the river. My friend Irene was telling me they like to hire more people for the summer, the younger people."

"We got hippies in Big Falls," I quickly say to James. "Some of them used to ride the school bus with us until they graduated like you. Jackie Gertz, Philly's friend, her sister, Terri. Terri got a job working at the sawmill."

Suddenly James puts on his round sunglasses and pulls his hair back behind his ears. He turns up his collar, then takes out his Kents from his front shirt pocket. He lights one up and leans back in his chair. "Hey, Mom?" he says, smiling, spotting my mother's new box of hair dye on the windowsill. "Let's drive up to International Falls tomorrow, just you and me."

My mother laughs a little, shaking her head.

"The Falls," I quickly say. "They just call it the Falls."

"Okay, Mom," James says. "Let's go to the Falls. I got plenty of graduation money left. We can go shopping, get something to eat, see a movie. They got a theater, right? Let's see *Cabaret*. I bet it's showing up there."

"You're gonna have to ask the old man if you can use his Oldsmobile," Scott says.

"He'll let me—if I buy him a pack of cigarettes," James says, reaching in his back pocket, pulling out his brown leather wallet. "Come on, Mom. Here's your chance to get away from the old man for a day—get away from all these papooses." He waits with the wallet in his hands until my mother laughs again, then he slaps down two twenties, three tens, and two fives on the table.

>[ ]<

As soon as Dennis and Joseph get home from working, they grab a loaf of bread and the leftover hamburgers. They head to the door and tell James to go with them to the loft. The day they came to haul away the Holstein cows, my father forgot to disconnect the electricity in the barn. Dennis and Joseph took an extension cord and stretched it up to the hayloft. They cleared a spot, painted three walls red, and found some junk couches at the dump. With money from their summer jobs, they bought a new stereo with a turntable with a diamond needle. Dennis said the only thing they needed to make the place as far out as it could get would be a black light. Joseph said he could make one by dipping a light bulb in a can of blue paint. It was cool the way the loft glowed purple. But pretty soon the bulb got too hot and exploded.

My mother tells me I am not going anywhere until she inspects the dishes. "What about Scott?" I say to her. "You know he just sneaked upstairs. Aren't you gonna call him?"

"Never mind about him," she says, looking over the plates and cups in the drain. She slides a plate back in the dishwater, then a handful of forks.

"Well, if you're gonna make me do all of those by myself, then I think I should be able to go with you and James to the Falls tomorrow."

"I'm not going anywhere," she says. "No one's going anywhere. We're broke."

"But James has money!" I say, picking up the dishrag. "I wanna see that movie he was talking about."

"You can't. It's R-rated."

"But I can get in if I'm with you!"

My mother holds up a plate for me to see. It's clean, but I know if I don't stop bugging her, she's going to make me wash all of the dishes all over again. She finally walks away from the dishes and opens the oven door. She tells me to take some of her cinnamon rolls out to the barn for Dennis and Joseph.

"We'll see a movie another time," she softly says. "When I get some money."

"When?" I say, rolling my eyes. "When you get your Indian payment check?" I finish the dish and forks, then toss the dishrag on the counter. I glare at my mother. "Even if your Indian check comes, you know the old man is just gonna drink it up."

Suddenly, out of the corner of my eye, I see my father limping into the kitchen. I wait for a few seconds, wondering if he heard me, if he's going to reach out and slap me across the face. He asks my mother if there's any butts left from any of James's cigarettes.

My mother holds out her cinnamon rolls wrapped in foil to me. "You wanna take these to your brothers, or do you wanna redo the dishes?"

Whiskey stays close to Scott and me as we pass the chicken coop. I know he wants to protect us from that rooster even though the chickens are already asleep. We can hear James and the older brothers talking the closer we get to the barn. James is laughing, yelling above his new Elton John album that's playing on the stereo. "That's no diamond needle! The sound's way too shitty, man!"

Just as we start climbing, Joseph sticks his head down at us. He reaches and points to Whiskey. "Hand him up here, you guys." We do like he wants, then he tells us to hand up the cinnamon rolls.

"Don't give them to him," Scott says. "Wait until he lets us up there."

"I'll let you guys up here," Joseph says. "Just give me the cinnamon rolls first."

Scott tells me again not to do it, but I hand up the cinnamon rolls anyway.

"Now, get back to the house, you little shits," Joseph says with a stupid smile on his big fat face.

"I knew you were gonna say that," Scott says.

"Okay, we'll go back to the house," I say. "But we're gonna tell the old man you're running the electricity. Let's go!"

But just as Joseph starts down the stairs to chase us, James calls for us to come back. "Get up here, you papooses! I wanna talk to you!" he says, laughing.

The hayloft is filled with smoke but not from cigarettes. John is sitting back on one of the beat-up couches, laughing. His eyes are wet.

"Are you guys sniffing glue?" Scott asks. "You know the old man doesn't like it when you sniff glue."

"Relax," James says. "It's just a little grass." He takes a puff, then passes it off to Dennis. "Now, come here. I wanna talk to you."

I sit on the sofa next to James. Joseph is gobbling up all the cinnamon rolls, sharing only the crumbs with Whiskey. Dennis switches records on the turntable. He holds one of James's albums, the cover a picture of a naked black woman looking at a red angel with blue wings floating over her head. James wants me to tell him about the hippies hanging out in Big Falls.

I ask him if I can look at his watch. "I didn't know hippies wore watches, not like this one," I say to him. "Is this real silver?"

He takes off his watch and holds it out for me. "Where do they hang out?"

"The Bible camp," I say, trying to snap the watch on my own wrist. "So did you bring us anything? You said you had something for us in your duffel bag."

"What's the Bible camp?" he asks.

I breathe out and shrug, giving the watch back. "I don't know. How come you're asking so many questions? The Bible camp is where everyone goes swimming down at the river. The hippies go there at night to drink beer. So since you didn't bring us anything, can you give us some money?"

James reaches in his shirt pocket and takes out his round sunglasses. He puts them on and leans his head back, smiling. "Who's that girl you mentioned back at the house?" he asks. "Philly's friend. What was her name? Terri?"

"Jackie is Philly's friend," I say, looking at his sunglasses. "Terri Gertz is Jackie's older sister. She's the one who works at the sawmill. Now, can I have some money?"

James says he'll think about it. I wait for an answer, but he doesn't say anything. He just sits there with those sunglasses on even though it's completely dark out now.

When Dennis turns off the stereo, he tells Scott and me that he has to go to sleep. "Gotta be uptown for work at seven AM," he says. "Hey, James? Get up. You got a bed made up at the house."

But James says he's staying right where he is. "For Christ's sake, Dennis," he says, laughing. "You're acting just like Frankie. Plastic, man! You're all just plastic!"

Dennis looks at me. I tap Scott on the shoulder. "We gotta go," I whisper. "James is gonna get crazy and start fighting."

"No, he's not. He's too high," Dennis says. "Joseph? John? Let's sleep in the house. James can stay here and fly all night if he wants."

Before we leave the barn, Dennis lights a match. He finds the electric box on the wall. He unscrews one of the fuses, and suddenly the music in the loft sounds like it's in slow motion until it dies out.

"What the hell's going on?!" James yells. "Turn it back on! What's the matter with you guys?"

Scott and I start running, but Dennis and the other brothers take their time, laughing as they walk back to the house.

"Get back here!" James yells from the silent, dark barn. "If you don't turn it back on, I'm gonna make you scrub floors and walls all day tomorrow!" He breaks out laughing again, laughter that we can hear all the way to the back porch of the house.

>[ ]<

When the old man's Oldsmobile leaves the driveway, taking Dennis and Joseph to work, I follow my mother to the barn. She steps over a broken milk stool and yells for James to get up. When he doesn't say anything, she tells me to climb up the ladder and wake him.

"He's gonna hit me because we turned off the electricity last night," I say. She quickly points up the ladder. Even though my mother hasn't used the broom on us in a really long time, I start climbing. When I reach the top of the ladder, I see that James is sitting up. He holds open his wallet, counting his money. He's still wearing his sunglasses.

"James? Mom wants to talk to you. She's downstairs. Dennis is the one who shut off the electricity, not me. And no, we didn't steal any of your money."

He smiles, and I slip back down the ladder.

My mother walks around the stalls where the old man used to milk his Holstein cows. She asks James if he could spare a few cigarettes for the old man. "He gets irritable when he can't smoke— hard to be around, you know?" She picks up a metal bucket and hangs it by its handle on a hook. She tells James that she would really like to spend a day in the Falls with him. She hasn't been to a movie theater since we left Milwaukee. "But things are pretty tight this time of the month. Running low on groceries."

James combs his long black hair and laughs. He asks how much the old man's bar tab is every month. She tells him groceries are expensive in a small town like Big Falls. "And those kids are getting bigger, eating more." My mother says she is up to baking eleven loaves of bread. "That bread is gone in two days. Every damn loaf."

James takes off his sunglasses and folds them in his hand. My mother says Dennis and Joseph are always willing to help out, but they don't get paid again for another two weeks. She bends down and picks up my father's broken milk stool. She wonders out loud if Dennis could nail some new legs on it. And then she wipes away dirt and dust from her hands and pulls on a loose thread dangling from the sleeve of her dress.

She tells James he is more than welcome to stay for as long as he wants. "They're used to Indians around these parts. It's the people from the city they don't trust. Or I could ask my friend Irene if she's got a relative in the Twin Cities you could stay with until you get a job, until you can save up for your place. If things go well, you might be able to even start college in the fall."

James nods and pulls out his wallet. He hands my mother two twenty-dollar bills. He tells her that he doesn't want to leave Big Falls. "I'm going to get a job at that sawmill. What do you think about that?" James flips open his sunglasses and slips them on. "And when I start saving up some good money, we'll take a trip together, Mom. We'll go to Minneapolis."

"That's fine," my mother says. "But you're going to have to go to sleep at night. Dennis and Joseph have to get up in the morning for work."

My mother wipes her neck and says it's going to be another humid day. She tells James they should drive up to the Falls and buy some groceries as soon as my father gets back from town, that there's no air conditioning in his Oldsmobile.

"Just you and me, Mom," James says. "Tell the old man I'll even fill it up."

But my mother looks at James in his eyes until he finally takes off his sunglasses. She says my father is going to do the driving. Then she turns to me. "We'll all go together."

⊰[13]⊱

Wounded Hearts

Ga-ween has become my mother's favorite Indian word this summer, especially since James bought her a new book on home remedies. Every chance she gets away from the stove, she turns on the fan full blast and lays on her bed to read about natural cures. We ask her if she has any extra change so we can walk uptown to go to the store. *Ga-ween*. We ask her if she can ask the old man to drive us to the dump so we can look for old radios, toys, or maybe some clothes for her. *Ga-ween*. We ask her if she can bake oatmeal cookies because we haven't had any in months. *Ga-ween*.

We're so sick and tired of her always telling us *ga-ween* that Philly finally blows up. "Mom! You're acting like a hypocrite. You never want to tell us any Indian words or anything about Chippewas. How can you say *ga-ween* all the time without getting a guilty conscience?"

My mother does not even look away from her book. She just lays there and mumbles, "Ever since you got back from that camp, you've become sassy as hell, Philly."

Philly storms out of the bedroom, saying she's going to town to see her friend Jackie. Sassy is only a small part of Philly's problem as far as I'm concerned. Now she's picky about what kind of jeans she wants to wear. She doesn't want bell-bottoms anymore. She wants flares. When James got paid for working at the sawmill, he bought her two really expensive pairs of jeans at Penney's just because she's the only girl in the family. What really drives me crazy is Philly telling me that I can't hang out with her and Jackie. She always stands on the dirt road looking back, threatening to throw rocks at me if I keep following her to town. And those few times that she does let me go with her to Jackie's house, she completely ignores me. Every time I sit next to them, they start whispering to each other. "You see how bored you are," she says. "Go find your own friends."

I would go to town on my own, but just like last summer, the twins, Rick and Robbie, are gone again, visiting cousins. The last time I hung out with Mike Hovan was on the Fourth of July. We were standing on the curb waiting for the parade to start, and he was telling me about how he was "damned determined" to hook up with Melissa Russell. "And if she says no again, I'm gonna slip this firecracker down her pants." But once my younger brothers and I started scrambling, shoving with all the other kids to get at the candy people were throwing from their parade floats, Mike disappeared in the crowd.

I sit on the edge of my mother's bed and think about bugging her about why I couldn't go with my father and the older brothers to Red Lake this morning. A few weeks ago while swimming in the creek about a mile down the dirt road from the farm, we spotted an old red wood canoe stuck on some rocks. Dennis talked my father into loading it on top of his Oldsmobile. They set the canoe on two sawhorses because it was waterlogged. My father spread layers of tar on the bottom to plug up the holes. When the final coat of red paint was dry, my father said he would take Dennis and the other older brothers fishing at Red Lake.

But I decide not to bug my mother because I know she'll just tell me to quit feeling sorry for myself. And that will make me blow up. I'll scream that I am not feeling sorry for myself. Then she'll remind me again that I need to start acting my age, that I'm going into the fourth grade now. Her bringing up school will just make me even madder because I'll see Mrs. Mattson standing in front of my desk with her arms folded, waiting for me to look up at the clock and tell the whole class what time it is.

So I don't say anything as I sit there on my mother's bed.

"What are you upset about?" I hear her asking.

"Nothing."

"Then quit kicking the bed."

I almost tell her that I'm not kicking the bed, but she switches the subject. "Why don't you go across the road and pick some more blueberries? James is bringing that bubbly girl, Terri, over for supper. I'll make some shortbread."

I get up and tell her Scott is upstairs, too busy reading comics to go with me. You have to go through some woods to get to an open field where the berries are growing. She tells me to take Whiskey.

"What's wrong with your memory?" I say. "They took Whiskey with them to Red Lake."

"What time is it?" she asks.

"I don't know, probably five o'clock."

"Oh, it is not. It couldn't be that late. You haven't learned how to tell time yet, have you?"

"Ga-ween, ga-ween," I say under my breath.

"You better start learning," she says, closing her book and sitting up. "You only have a few more weeks. That Mrs. Mattson says she's going to test you when you go back to school."

I try not to blow up. I try to sound normal. "Well, I can't learn to snap my fingers or whistle, either. What's she gonna do? Flunk me before the first day is even over?"

My mother moves to the door, telling me to bring her fan. I don't do like she wants. In the kitchen, she says if I don't want to pick blueberries, then she wants me to go out to the garden and get her some fresh corn. She leaves the room. I stare at the empty ice cream bucket on the floor by the back door. When she returns with her fan, I wait until she plugs it in, until it starts cooling her off as she digs for her baking pans. "I can't get the corn," I calmly say. "What if that rooster comes after me?"

"Oh, for Pete's sake!" my mother says. "You're almost ten years old. Stand up to that rooster. Hit him with the bucket!"

"What are you so mad about?" I say.

"Because you're not acting your age, that's what. You can't expect to be hanging around your sister all the time. You gotta stop being afraid of the dark. And believe me, I'm through listening to your whining and pouting!"

"I'm not pouting!"

"Now, get the hell outside. You're bugging me!"

I kick the bucket out the door and jump down the steps. As soon as I pick it up, I see the rooster coming toward me. I make a break for the garden, thinking I can hide in the tall cornstalks. I glance back and see the rooster trying to catch up with me. When I reach the garden, I slip through the stalks and stand in a middle row. I look for the rooster, but he isn't coming to get me. I know where he is. He's standing on the edge of the garden, waiting. That's what he does. He waits for me. I remember being stuck in the barn all morning once because that rooster refused to leave. He just clucked around, picking at hay and corncobs, waiting for me to come down.

But I am not going to stay in the garden all afternoon. I look past the fence and see the old, rusting, green station wagon that my father bought for thirty dollars at an auction. He bought that car when he figured he couldn't afford to fix the Oldsmobile after it broke down. But that station wagon barely made it back to the farm. He couldn't get it started again, so he junked it in the field. Scott, Michael, and I sometimes pretend the station wagon is a secret cave, a hideout from the Indians. When we play, I always grab the broken BB gun that used to be John's, and Scott and Michael pull out the cracked squirt guns we found at the dump. And then we make a break for it, riding our horses, shooting at the Indian warriors all the way back to the house. Pretending to fight Indians never lasts very long. Scott always quits as soon as we get back to the yard. He wants a turn with the BB gun, but I tell him he's not as good a shot as I am.

I decide to come back later to get the corn from the garden, and I climb over the fence. I place the empty bucket on the hood and see the BB gun on the front seat. I grab it, climb on top of the car, and watch for the rooster in case he dares to come after me.

>[ ]<

I figure it must be at least five o'clock by now. I had dozed off for awhile, until the hood of the station wagon felt too hot to stay on. I grab the bucket with one hand and carry the BB gun with me just in case I need to clobber that rooster. I circle around the farm, through the fields. I sit in the shade of the tractor my father borrowed from Merle Mac. It's been in the field all summer because it ran out of gas.

I don't take my break for too long. I know my mother is wondering where in the hell I ran off to. And I figure she'll really be upset with me for having to pick the corn herself. I lift up the bottom of my shirt and wipe away the sweat burning my eyes, then start back. I don't care anymore if she blows up at me. She might reach out and slap me or grab me by my ear, but at least she won't take the broom after me. My mother doesn't do that anymore.

The first thing that comes to my mind once I get to the edge of the yard is that I should have left the BB gun in the field. James is staring, smiling at me through the big picture window. He thinks I've been playing in the field all afternoon. I don't want him telling me I should start acting my age. As soon as he disappears, I toss the gun under one of the pine trees.

When I get to the house, he is waiting for me, sitting on the back porch steps.

"Where's your girlfriend?" I say.

"Where's the corn?" he says, still smiling, eating a slice of watermelon.

"Where'd you get that?" I ask.

"The Red Owl," he says.

I look past him through the open door and see Terri Gertz sitting at the kitchen table with my mother, cutting up the watermelon. I can't hear her laughing because the stereo is blaring the Carole King album. When James brought that album home the same day he and Philly shopped for her jeans and bought my mother that medicine book, I studied the cover and thought Carole King looked just like Terri—long curly hair, bright blue jeans, and bare feet.

James goes up the porch steps, and I know he's going to tell my mother there is no corn. But the real reason why I quickly walk toward the garden is that I don't want to be around when James tells Terri I'm too old to be playing like I was this afternoon.

In the garden, I snap corn from stalks. James slips through the rows, finding me. He holds out a piece of watermelon, saying the Red Owl got a big truckload today. Normally I would have stood up and walked away, but I can't remember the last time we had watermelon. We tried growing some in the garden. My father let John order seeds last spring. He said it would be a long shot, that there may not be enough warm days this far north for watermelons to grow.

"So how many Indians did you kill today?" he asks just before he laughs at me.

James teases more than anyone else in the family, almost non-stop. Sometimes he goes too far. At night he likes to wait until I'm alone upstairs or in the basement. And then he switches off the light and starts making ghost sounds. If I didn't scream as loud as I do, my mother would never get after him. I can never tell how serious James is because he always smiles, even when he's bossing us around the kitchen. But when I glance up from the corn bucket, he is no longer smiling.

"So I hear you've been pissing off the old lady," James says.

"Old lady? Why you calling Mom an old lady?"

"It's what hippies say."

"You mean plastic hippies."

I finish eating the slice of watermelon, then toss the green rind over the fence. James smiles again and pulls his long hair into a ponytail to wipe sweat from the back of his neck.

"Why you always buying Philly new clothes?" I ask. "Now Scott is bragging you're going to take him shopping for school clothes. Why? Because he stutters?"

I glance at him and see he is no longer smiling. I turn away, hiding my face behind a cornstalk because sometimes, maybe even worse than his scaring me, he forces me into having one of his "talks." I don't like it at all when he tries to get me to memorize what he wants me to say to Mrs. Mattson once school starts again. I'm not gonna argue with Mrs. Mattson about President Nixon. I can't remember everything he says I should say to her except that Nixon is the most crooked president we ever had. When he wants to talk to me about why I need to start watching the TV news to learn about what's going on in the world so I can disagree with Mrs. Mattson, I just shake my head. I watched the news one night, and when it was over, I still couldn't figure out what was really going on in Vietnam.

"Maybe I should buy you a book I read in high school," he says, still not smiling. "It's about Indians. *Bury My Heart at Wounded Knee.*"

I've never heard of that book, but I know I wouldn't want to read it because of that word "wounded." It makes me feel bad about how hard it is for my mother, makes me feel ashamed about living poor like we are, how we have to put up with a drunk white father.

"It was a cold winter in 1890 on the plains of South Dakota," James says, looking past the rows of corn to the edge of the fields. "There was a massacre of women, old men, and children."

The warm wind kicks up dust in my face. I move closer to the swaying cornstalks, hoping the sound of their whipping leaves will drown out what he's going to say next, that an army of cowboys killed those Indians. But I *do* hear him telling me about the smoke of guns, the burning bullets, the blood dripping from the backs of those Indian women, old men, and children as they tried to run away. I rub the dirt from my eyes, hoping to block out the pictures of those dead women, old men, and children lying face down in the cold winter of Wounded Knee.

I step further away from my brother's story and try to imagine myself at school, in Mrs. Mattson's fourth-grade class. I want to raise my hand so I can say something to Mrs. Mattson about President Nixon. But when she calls on me, the only thing I can think to say is that I will never, ever play cowboys and Indians again.

⟩[14]⟨

A Magic Hat

About a mile away from home, Lynnette Meas gets up from her seat and storms to the back of the bus. She sticks her finger in Gale Nygard's face and tells her she'd better repent.

"What does that mean?" I whisper to my sister.

And then Lynnette orders Gale to ask God for forgiveness.

"For what?" I say to Philly.

But my sister does not have to explain any of it to me because Lynnette does for everyone on the school bus. "For the one-hundredth time, Gale! Square dancing is a sin!"

Something happened to Lynnette and her older brother, Randall, over the summer. They became Jesus freaks. That's what Philly said they were. For the past month, the Meases have been telling everyone on the bus that we have to be "born again" and only Jesus can save us from our sins. But Gale doesn't agree.

"Square dancing is not a sin!" Gale yells back at Lynnette. "The worst we do is hold hands!"

"Dancing leads to other sins—drugs and fornication!"

I would ask my sister what that last word means, but I don't want to know. It sounds worse than a swear word.

Once the bus doors close behind us, I look back and see Lynnette's finger still wagging at Gale, her mouth wide open and her teeth like fangs.

I call for Philly to wait up because I want to ask her how that fight got started. She bends down and rubs Whiskey's ears. My sister is in the same grade as Lynnette and Gale. She explains that their fifth-grade teacher, Mr. Reese, has been teaching the class how to square dance during phy ed.

"Did you square dance today?" I ask her.

"Yep, but Lynnette didn't say a word to me about it being a sin."

"How come?"

"Gale wears hot pants. I guess wearing hot pants is another sin."

I take off running to catch up with John, who is almost to the house. I can't remember if Canada and Russia played in the final game of their hockey series while we were in school today. This week they've been playing in Russia, which means it's dark there and daylight here.

"They play tomorrow," John says.

"Are you gonna skip school so you can watch it?" I ask.

But John puts his finger to his lips and looks up at the kitchen window, which is open. I hear a stranger's voice once John opens the back door into the kitchen. Whiskey slips past us. He doesn't bark at the stranger, who is leaning against the wall with his arms folded. He must have been here for awhile, long enough for Whiskey to get used to him.

The stranger is a skinny white hippie, about James's age, I figure. He has long brown hair that hangs past his shoulders and a brown beard but no mustache. And he holds a shiny black hat in his hands.

He smiles and holds out a hand to John. My mother pours a glass of orange Kool-Aid. My father digs through his milk can filled with his papers. Some of them are spread out on the table.

I look back at the stranger and see him smiling at me with his hand out. I shake it, then notice how long his beard is, how it stretches past his neck and down his red and blue tie-dye shirt. When Philly and the other brothers come inside, he smiles and shakes each of their hands. I ask him what kind of hat he's wearing.

"It's a fedora," he says. "It's made of fur felt."

"Are you a friend of James?" Philly asks.

He nods and turns to my mother, who is holding out the Kool-Aid glass. He smiles at her and says thanks. He looks at all of us. "God, what a tribe," he says with a laugh.

His name is Michael Stoops. He drove up here from Duluth. James and his girlfriend, Terri, met Michael sometime in the summer at the Bible camp. Michael tells us he thinks Big Falls is far out as he takes out a pair of wire-rimmed glasses from his leather briefcase that bulges with papers.

Michael decided to come back for a visit because James invited him. But he didn't know James moved to Minneapolis two weeks ago. James got tired of living in Big Falls, working at the sawmill. Terri went with him. James sent my mother a postcard with a picture of the new tall, blue glass building they built in downtown Minneapolis. On the back, he wrote that he found a one-room apartment near the university and that he had a good job lead working as an assistant at one of the radio stations. He also wrote that Terri was catching the Greyhound back home because the city was too fast, too loud. He wrote. "It's turning her into a nervous wreck, ha! ha!"

My father stands up and steps over to the other end of the table where Michael is now sitting with his glasses on. My father hands him some stapled papers and says something about the farm payments being too high. Michael reads and flips through each page. My father says he would like to get those payments lowered if at all possible.

My mother tells us to scatter.

I don't get to see much of the cartoons on TV because I keep turning around, looking back toward the kitchen. At the dinner table, Michael Stoops eats macaroni and tomato sauce but not with hamburger. My mother made him a separate batch because he told her he never eats meat. We don't get to ask Michael a lot of questions because my father hogs the conversation. He asks Michael if he grew up in an Amish family because of the shape of his beard. But Michael says he was raised Quaker.

"I'm no longer practicing," he says. "But I am still very much a pacifist."

"Well, even a lot of religious fanatics are opposed to what's going on in Vietnam," my father says.

As soon as there is a silent second, I jump in and ask Michael why he has so many papers in his briefcase. He's studying to be a lawyer. He went to college to be a social worker, and now he wants to work for the rights of poor people. He says the justice system favors rich people. Then he wipes his mouth and laughs again. "Now, let me ask you a question," he says. "Do you think the Canadians are going to beat the Russians?"

Before it gets dark, Scott and I follow my father and Michael around the farm. Michael wears his black hat and smokes one of my father's rolled cigarettes. My father points around the cleared fields. He says that he'd like to save money to plant five acres of oats and that he knows a farmer in Northome who might be interested in paying him a fair price to grow hay in the rest of the fields.

My father flicks his cigarette in the dewy grass and asks Michael if he's planning on staying for a few days.

Michael takes off his hat and begins rubbing the shiny fur. "I'm actually taking this quarter to study on my own," Michael says. "I'll enroll again in November."

"Stay with us," my father says. "Stay as long you like. You can have James's old bedroom. It's got a door and a lock, so you can study in peace."

Michael shakes my father's hand and slaps him on the shoulder. Before we head back to the house, Michael rubs his hat one more time before putting it back on his head.

>[ ]<

Last night, I finally made up my mind that I was not going to school this morning. I decided I would get sick and have to stay home, rest on the couch with a clear view of the TV. It's the only way I can see the final hockey game between Canada and Russia.

John is excited to go to school today because they are going to wheel a TV into his classroom and watch the game. Mrs. Mattson couldn't care less about hockey. She told us her reason for not letting us watch the game was more than just her "staunch conviction" that sports had no place in the classroom. She's "very leery" about technology. Mrs. Mattson is worried that one of these days, technology will replace teachers. She believes we're becoming too dependent on technology in our everyday lives. She says if the cost of gas ever hits forty cents a gallon, she's going to take that as a sign that it's time to "drop out of the human race." Mrs. Mattson is going to trade in her Chevrolet Impala for a horse and buggy.

But when I come down the stairs and see my mother opening a new bag of brown sugar, I don't know if I can get away with complaining that I have a stomachache. We hardly ever get to have brown sugar with our oatmeal. I end up eating two bowls before someone yells that the bus is coming.

Once I get outside, Joseph grabs me by the shirt collar. I suddenly remember that he was going to pay me back for drawing on some of his good paper. I only stole a couple of sheets, but Scott squealed on me because he was paying me back for stealing some of his gum that he was too greedy to share. Joseph kicks me, then pushes me to the ground. He runs off to the bus, and I feel my eyes filling up with tears. Even if I can stop crying, I can't get on the bus now because everyone will know. And I can't say anything to my mother about Joseph beating me up because she'll say I must have had it coming.

I get up and wipe my eyes on my sleeve, then brush off gravel from the side of my pants. Suddenly I do feel sick, sick enough to hold my hand on my stomach and limp back inside the house.

My mother does not ask what's wrong. She just tells me that's what I get for pouring so much brown sugar on my oatmeal. She tells me to go back to bed, that maybe my stomach will feel better by noon.

I know I shouldn't do it, but I steal more of Joseph's good drawing paper, and I sit in bed with his new Avengers comic.

I spend the whole morning drawing until I hear the television. My father has been looking forward to watching the hockey game because he served in World War II. He believes General Patton was right when he said we should go to war with the Russians.

When I get downstairs with my pillow, I force a little cough and ask my mother if I can have the couch. She opens the refrigerator and says she got a ride into town with Michael Stoops this morning and bought a can of 7UP for me. Michael wanted to see if he could find an ink ribbon for his typewriter at the hardware store. I hear Michael's voice coming from the living room, telling my father that he can't believe how much they charge for basic supplies and what little selection they offer. "People in this town ought to organize a boycott," he says. "People shouldn't have to drive forty miles to get a fair deal on soap and shoes. Capitalism in a small town, Don. I'm telling you, this country is screwin' over the poor man!"

But Michael forgets about how expensive it can be to live in Big Falls when the Canadians score their first goal. Even my mother comes into the living room to see Michael jumping in the air and clapping his hands.

My mother has never watched even a minute of any hockey game in the past. But today, she sits in front of the TV, holding onto Robert's hands as he stands between her legs. She even sighs and waves her hand at the Russian judges for taking too long to turn on the red goal light when the Canadians tie the game in the third period.

Our living room turns quiet. Michael rubs his hat and says the Russians will be declared the winners if the game ends in a tie. The Russians scored more goals than the Canadians during the entire series. But it doesn't come down to that. The Canadians score the winning goal during the final minute of the game.

My mother says she's in the mood to make a cake. I watch her get up with her bowl of cut carrots and see her smiling. That smile lasts for the rest of the day. And I'm not sure why I feel the same way. Maybe it's because after living as long as we have in Big Falls, after watching so much Canadian TV and listening all day to the radio station that comes out of Fort Frances, we are more Canadian than American.

She spreads white frosting across the top of her cake, and I look into her smile. "Do you wish you were Canadian and not Indian, Mom?" I ask.

She bursts out laughing and asks me how in the world a hockey game could ever make me think of that question.

I tell her I have no idea, but could I lick the bowl when she's finished?

⋇[ ]⋇

Michael Stoops spends almost all of his time in his room upstairs. He has a card table filled with his schoolbooks, papers, and typewriter. Even on the weekends, we hardly see him. But at night he comes downstairs and watches TV with my parents. He's convinced President Nixon is more than "corrupt" because of that Watergate stuff.

Some nights after supper, Michael helps my dad with trying to figure out how much he has to spend for his oats and how much he can expect to grow and sell. Or how to fill out some government forms that came in the mail that day. Michael sits with my dad at the kitchen table, picking through the last pieces of Halloween candy, leftovers like Sweet Tarts and candy corn. He reads the directions on what to write so my father can order Social Security cards for each of us.

My mother comes into the kitchen with her sweater on. She calls Whiskey and opens the back door.

Michael looks up at her, taking off his glasses, smiling. "It's pretty chilly out there, Corrine."

"Oh, I won't be out long," she says. "It's starting to get dark."

We watch her and the dog disappear. Michael puts down the Social Security forms and rubs his hat. I stare at him, wondering what he's going to say after he's thought about it long enough. He does that a lot. We ask him questions about why he gave up being a Quaker and if he still believes in God. He takes off his hat and rubs it for a minute or so before coming up with an answer or sometimes asking us a question back.

"What you thinking, Michael?" my father asks.

"Are your kids enrolled in their mother's tribe?"

My father shrugs and reaches for his tobacco and papers. "I used to mention it to Corrine, tell her she should write to Bad River," my father says. "But she never makes the time. The last time I brought it up, she almost bit my head off—said something like, 'Why? What does it matter? There's nothing for them in Odanah.'"

My father offers the cigarette to Michael, then rolls another one. Michael strikes a match and gets up. He puts his hands behind his back and looks out the window. I know he is watching my mother. "Well, that might be true, no future at Bad River. I don't know. It's not for me to say. But, Don? Tribal enrollment is a legal right. Those kids are heirs to her land. Corrine should know that."

Michael Stoops takes one more drag, then reaches for his hat. He looks at my father and waits for him to say, "Yes, please, speak with her."

I know my father won't let me follow Michael outside, so I go to the window. I can't see my mother from this angle, but I know she's standing in the driveway under the yard light. Michael disappears under the yard light, too. But I can see his shadow. It's taller than he is. Even his black hat is bigger. I watch for a few more minutes until I see the large shadow of his hand reach out to my mother. I know she takes it. I know she is saying yes, she agrees that it's a good idea to write to Bad River, a very important thing to do. And I know Michael is saying he will help her with the letter. He'll bring his typewriter downstairs and sit with her at the kitchen table. He will rub his black hat and stare at the blank sheet of paper. And then it will come to him. Michael will know exactly what to write for my mother.

This Christmas Morning

Dear Frankie,

Sorry for not writing back sooner, but things have been pretty hectic around here the past few months. I'm glad to hear that you and Germaine decided to wait until next December before getting married. Maybe you'll be able save up some money after graduating next spring. You don't want to go into a marriage broke, believe me.

But I'm going to come for a visit before then. I got another letter from Odanah in the mail. The tribe apologized for such a long delay in getting back to me about the status of my land payment. I guess that's what you call bureaucracy. They asked me to continue to please be patient. It sounds like the check will be sent in a few months. Don said the same thing, to be patient. I sure would like to come the day I get paid, but I can't leave Don with the kids while they're in school. I'll have to wait until the end of May or early June.

It's funny. I had all but given up on ever receiving that payment. I did give up on ever getting the chance to visit you and the sisters. Every time I try to save a few dollars from selling eggs, I have to spend it on things that come up like tennis shoes and gym outfits for the older boys in high school. Last week, Philly begged me to buy her a pair of ice skates. We had a lot of rain this fall that left a pond behind the barn. I found her a decent pair at the Salvation Army in the Falls (International Falls).

Like I say, I had given up on that land payment. But last fall, that nice law school student who stayed with us (I wrote to you about him) helped me get all you kids enrolled in Bad River. You should be getting your tribal ID in the mail soon. Anyway, after we did that, I showed him the original land papers I received from the tribe. He reached for a new sheet of paper and typed another letter on my behalf.

All of that happened in early November. He said he had to get back to Duluth. School was starting again. Dennis helped him load up his car with his books and typewriter. I packed him up some egg sandwiches and caramel rolls, which I never make because the ingredients cost so much. I don't know if we'll ever see him again. I hope so, but it's a long drive this far north. If you and Germaine ever get a chance to drive up here, you'll see just how far away we are from the rest of the world.

But I actually have settled in some here in Big Falls. The kids don't get on my nerves like they used to. When James was here last summer, he got after them to stop their roughhousing and eating in the living room, leaving their dishes and candy wrappers everywhere. Don is behaving, too. He still drinks but keeps to himself most of the time. He hasn't bugged me about using my Indian check to pay for some oats he wants to plant in the summer. We'll see. The only thing I know for sure is that I am going to buy a bus ticket.

I haven't heard from James in quite awhile. He called my friend Irene Cloutier on Thanksgiving. Sounds like he is still working at a radio station in Minneapolis. He and Irene talked for quite awhile, but he said he'd have to write me a long letter because it's pretty tough to try and plan on being at Irene's waiting for a call—and expensive.

Speaking of Thanksgiving, we had more visitors. Don brought home a couple from the Nett Lake Reservation. Delma and Lonnie got stuck

at the tavern uptown one night. Their ride took off, I guess. And then
we had one of our famous blizzards. Delma helped me cook the meal.
When the roads cleared, Don offered to drive them home. Nett Lake is
only a little over an hour from here. But he came home early. Delma and
Lonnie wanted to stop off at the bar and have a drink. Later I told Don
he'd better get up there and bring the both of them back to the farm
because it gets very cold at night up here. But when he got to the bar, they
were already gone.

How's Jerry doing? You wrote in your last letter that he isn't working.
Is he still hanging around those Sawicki brothers? I suppose he should
think about coming up here before he gets into big trouble. Of course,
he'll have to find work if he does come to Big Falls. Maybe he could get
a job at the mill like James did. It's about the only thing he could do. Jerry
wouldn't last a half day in the woods. That's hard work and dangerous.
Don was at the gas station a few weeks ago. He overhead some men talking about one of the lumberjacks, a bachelor who got crushed to death by
the tree he was cutting down. Another guy got his chest all cut up when
the chain on his saw snapped. Even if Don wasn't disabled, I wouldn't
want him doing that kind of work. I'd be a nervous wreck if he did.

I sure hope that check does come soon. I've been thinking about the
sisters this morning. Growing up, there wasn't much for any of us under
the Christmas tree, but we always had a big meal and each other. I've
been trying to tell that to the kids all week. Sure, it would be nice to go
on a big Christmas shopping spree for everyone, but we're poor. It's as
simple as that. But at least they've got a warm house and a twenty-five-
pound turkey to eat.

It'll be daylight soon. Pretty soon those kids will come banging down
the stairs. I was hoping to write your Aunt Sylvia this morning. Oh, I
exchanged cards with her and the other sisters and Don's mother, but
I want to write Sylvia back because she wrote that she was thinking of

trying to get Philomena and Victoria to drive up here sometime after the new year. I had to laugh when she asked if forty below was as cold as it sounds. I'll have to write her later tonight or tomorrow and let her know that I will be coming down once school lets out. I wouldn't want them to try and drive up here. They'll end up in the ditch. That can happen in a split second if you don't know how to drive on these roads.

Once the oven's preheated, I'll get the turkey inside. Then I'm going to take the dog out. I haven't looked at the thermometer, but I know it's well below zero. Thank God I found this long wool coat when I was at the Salvation Army. I also bought a decent pair of gloves. None of the kids know I have them. I keep them hidden under my mattress.

It's going to be another long winter in northern Minnesota. We'll start butchering many of the chickens next month. All that scalding and plucking should keep my mind off the snow and cold. I do have to admit that I enjoy the sunrise. Even when the kids are raising hell with each other, fighting over what clothes to wear or where to sit at the breakfast table, I like to just stare out the big picture window. The whole house lights up. The sun shines long after the kids have caught the bus.

I'll continue to check the mail every morning, looking for that check. It'll be good to see you and Germaine. You're going to think I'm crazy, but the more excited I get about coming down there for my visit, the more I start missing Don and the kids. Can you believe that? I'm already thinking about the bus ride back to Big Falls.

Merry Christmas!

Love, your mother.

$\gg\!\big[\,1973\,\big]\!\ll$

❧[16]❧

Young Summers

Philly says if I don't wear something green for school today, no one will know I'm part Irish. But like always, she's wearing one of my only good shirts, a green turtleneck with yellow stripes. Of course she lies about it, tries to tell me she picked it out first from some rummage sale we went to last summer. "Besides, it's a girl's shirt anyway," she says, storming down the hall.

"How can you tell that?" I yell just as she reaches the top of the stairs.

"Because it used to be Louise Smith's."

"That's another lie!"

She turns around and puts her hands on her hips. "Every time you wear it, she starts laughing at you behind your back." Philly stares at me until I'm sure she can see my face turning hot red. Finally she rolls her eyes and starts racing down the stairs.

I go inside the bedroom and sit on the edge of the mattress. I try not to look out the window because I know the gray clouds are just glaring at me. I wish Philly had never said anything to me about that snotty Louise Smith. I wish she would have told Louise Smith that it only looked like the shirt she used to own, that my mother bought me the same green turtleneck with yellow stripes at Penney's.

I hear my mother calling up the stairs for me "to get a move on!" But the only green thing I can find to wear from the pile of clothes in the closet is some corduroy pants. I can't remember if they came from a rummage sale or not. I fling the corduroys across the room and wonder why we're even celebrating St. Patrick's Day in school today when it really comes on a Saturday this year.

I have only enough time to spread some margarine on my piece of toast before the bus turns off the highway down our dirt road. My mother takes a pound of frozen hamburger out of the refrigerator and laughs when Dennis asks her if she thinks he could convince his teachers that he's really Irish and not Indian. I turn around and see Dennis pretending to scrub away the dark skin from his arms. He acts like one of the nun teachers my mother used to have at St. Mary's on the reservation. "Come on, Corrine! Scrub that dirt away until your skin is as white as the altar!" My mother has to cover her mouth. She gets embarrassed whenever she laughs too loud.

But as I take one last bite of my toast, watching everyone run to the door for the bus, I don't burst out laughing like my mother and Dennis. I just check to make sure there are no crumbs sticking to my blue shirt.

On the bus, I can hear Philly behind me, bragging about being part Irish to someone. I don't know who, since I can't even stand to look at my sister. I think about whacking her over the head with my social studies book. But that only makes me remember the assignment I was supposed to work on last night—reading a chapter on Minnesota's government and writing down the answers to a bunch of questions. The last time I missed turning in this much homework, Mrs. Mattson asked why I never bothered to do it, and I shrugged my shoulders. She didn't like that answer, so she yanked hard on my left ear to prove it. I don't know why Mrs. Mattson didn't just become a nun.

Before I know it, everyone is rushing off the bus and onto the playground. I see that chubby Louise Smith wearing a red, puffy coat with a green hat and mittens. She doesn't look Irish to me. She looks like she's related to one of Santa's elves. Even though most of the snow is melted and the temperatures are getting warmer, the monitor, Mrs. Olson, tells us we can play inside the gym before school starts. I know there will be dodgeball, my favorite, but I can't get chewed out again by Mrs. Mattson. I have to try and finish at least some of my social studies questions.

She doesn't notice me as I slip in the classroom and find my desk toward the back of the room. Mrs. Mattson is holding a math book and writing on the blackboard. I open my social studies book and turn to a clean page in my notebook. She is wearing a dark green skirt and a pinkish scarf around her neck. I don't know if she is Irish, and I don't want to ask. The first bell is going to ring in about fifteen minutes if I read the clock on the wall correctly.

"That's a good-looking shirt you're wearing," I hear Mrs. Mattson saying. I look up from my desk and see her still at the blackboard, finding a spot in her book with her index finger. "Blue looks good on you, Mr. Rolo."

I lean over my social studies book and put my hand over the blank notebook page.

"Is your father Irish?" she asks without looking at me.

"Yes, a little. But he's mostly French."

Mrs. Mattson sets down her chalk, closes her math book, and walks to her desk. She glances up at the clock, then pulls out her black purse from the bottom drawer. I hope she goes down the hall to the teacher's lounge. My friend Mike Hovan says she is a big-time chain smoker, that she likes to sit in the lounge and have two or three cigarettes before class and the same during lunch hour. I close my eyes and hope she is in the mood for at least ten cigarettes. When I open my eyes, she is still in the room. She unwraps a butterscotch candy and slips it in her mouth. She lowers her face and looks at me from above her brown-rimmed glasses.

"Do you ever watch the news on TV?" she asks.

"Sometimes," I say, looking back down at my book. "But it's mostly about Canada. We only get the one channel from Winnipeg."

"There's a big story in the news about some Indian protestors in South Dakota," she says, standing up and then slowly walking toward me. "Have you heard about it?"

I catch myself from shrugging and instead tell her yes, I know about those Indians protesting.

She doesn't say anything. I think she knows I'm lying. She leans on the edge of the desk in front of me, puts her hands in her lap, and carefully folds the butterscotch wrapper until it's the size of a rock-hard shirt button.

"The Indians have really big protest signs," I say, hoping she'll believe that.

"They have guns, Mr. Rolo," she says.

I start writing in my notebook, just copying words from my social studies book, words I'm not even reading.

"Mr. Rolo?" she says, pointing at my social studies book. "Those discussion questions are due today, aren't they?"

I start to mumble about my baby brother scribbling on my homework last night with a crayon, but Mrs. Mattson raises her index finger to her lips and glares at me.

"Now, listen up, Mr. Rolo," she softly says. "I want you to watch the news this weekend. Come Monday morning, I want you to give us an oral report on the Indian standoff in South Dakota. I don't want to hear any excuses about why you're not prepared to give us that report. Don't even bother coming to school if you don't have it done. Do you understand me, Mr. Rolo?"

I nod my head.

"I said, do you understand me, Mr. Rolo?"

"Yes, I do. I do understand you, Mrs. Mattson."

⊰[ ]⊱

Joseph has plans to ride along with my father to the Falls tomorrow. He's going to buy a new pad of drawing paper and some comic books, depending on how much money he can get from my father. Joseph says he's got at least twenty-five bucks coming. That's how much he lent my father when he was making money from his summer job. "It's going on eight months, and the old man still hasn't paid me back," he says, waiting for me to spread out the last sheet of white meat paper on the dining room table. "I can't draw on this shit. I need some decent paper."

But Scott and I watch as he takes the pair of rusty scissors and cuts around the dried blood spots. We had the last of the hamburger with macaroni for dinner. My mother told my father he would have to see if he has enough to pick up some tomato paste and chili powder because we ran out of that, too.

Joseph opens up pages of a *Sports Illustrated* magazine he checked out from the high school library, then sharpens his pencil with the kitchen knife. Even though he hates drawing on meat wrapping, it's at least better than drawing on notebook paper with lines. We watch as he flips through pages, looking for the right football picture to draw. He doesn't like Bob Griese and the rest of the Miami

Dolphins for winning the Super Bowl this year. He plans on changing the Dolphins' helmet and uniform to the Vikings or Baltimore Colts in his drawing.

We sit at the table with Joseph until my father says it's time to turn on the news. Joseph drops his pencil and gets up, saying he can't concentrate with the TV blaring. "What time we leaving tomorrow?" he says as my father stands by the television, waiting for it to warm up. "You're gonna give me the rest of the money you owe me, right?"

My father doesn't say anything back to Joseph. Instead he tells me to go into the kitchen and get his can of tobacco. Joseph slams his chair against the table and stomps out of the room. He knows there's no point in trying to argue with my father. He knows we don't have twenty-five dollars this time of the month, not until the first. The only reason my father is going to the Falls tomorrow is that his friend Merle Mac has to pick up some blood pressure medicine at the Rexall drugstore and he wanted someone to ride along.

When I get into the kitchen, Joseph is digging through the refrigerator, looking for leftovers. My mother is standing by the sink with a dish towel hanging over her shoulder and a diaper pin between her lips. I don't know if her hair is just sweaty or if she just finished washing it. Sometimes my mother washes her hair in the sink. I reach for my father's tobacco on the shelf above the stove, then watch her pin a tear in her dress back together. Joseph closes the refrigerator door and wants to know "who in the hell ate the rest of the macaroni and hamburger." My mother breathes out and wipes her face and head with the towel. Suddenly Joseph opens the refrigerator door and slams it shut, trying to get my mother's attention. But she does not even look at him. She just hangs the towel over her shoulder and puts her hands around the back of her neck and slowly walks out of the kitchen.

She tells Whiskey to scoot over and make room for her so she can sit down on the couch to watch the news. She reaches for the arm of the couch and takes a big sigh as she slowly sits down. I give my father the almost-empty can of Prince Albert tobacco, then go back to the dining room table. Scott and I take turns filling in the uniforms to finish my brother's football drawing until, just like Joseph, I realize I can't concentrate with the TV blaring, either. I decide to go upstairs and listen to the radio if Joseph isn't too mad to let me in the bedroom. With summer coming, we won't be able to pick up WLS, a rock station in Chicago, at night anymore. We can tune it in only during the winter. Not even Dennis can figure out how we are able to hear a radio station from Chicago when we're living this far north.

Just as I turn away from the table, I hear the name of a place that I have heard of before coming from the TV. Wounded Knee, South Dakota. I look into the living room, past the rising smoke of my father's rolled cigarette, past my mother's staring eyes, and I see Indians holding guns on the television screen. I see Indians wearing jean jackets and bandannas on their heads of braided hair, guarding an old, small church. A torn American flag is flapping in the wind. The Indians are surrounded by miles of brown, rolling hills filled with white men who have bigger guns and tanks.

I try to listen to learn what the fighting is about, but the story is already over. The newsman comes back on and then a commercial, a spring sale going on at a department store in downtown Winnipeg. I could ask my father to tell me about the Indians protesting with guns in Wounded Knee. I should tell him that I need to get out my notebook and write down the details so I can give a report to my class on Monday morning.

"The Indians really mean business," my father says. I look at my mother. She is smiling to herself, softly stroking Whiskey's head in her lap.

"What do the Indians call themselves, Corrine? The American Indian Movement?"

She only nods, still smiling.

The light from the television flickers. My mother's eyes sparkle. I think she must feel the way she used to when she was a little girl, when her hands weren't so hard, dry, and cracked, when her hair was long, flowing black silk and her brown skin was smooth all the way down to the bottoms of her feet. I wonder if that's the same smile she had as a girl when she came home from the last day of school at St. Mary's, untying the laces of her polished shoes, tossing them under her bed, unsnapping the tight buttons of her white blouse and picking up a faded T-shirt lying on the floor of the closet. How loud my mother must have laughed as she ran barefoot through the rain and mud during those young summers. She must have stretched out under the sweaty sun all day until her skin turned as pure brown as the Earth.

❖[17]❖

A View from Fields

I get to leave home just in the nick of time. Last night my other older brother Jerry showed up at the farm when my mother was helping me pack for camp. He never even sent a letter to let us know. Dennis just happened to be uptown cashing his check at the Red Owl when he saw him getting out of a chip truck, waving goodbye to the driver. When Jerry walked in the house in his brand-new leather shoes, tight jeans, and a yellow silk shirt that showed off his chest, my mother asked where his bags were.

Jerry smiled and clapped his hands. "You're looking at it."

She told me to hold my finger on the knot while she tied some twine around the cardboard box filled with my camp clothes. "So you're broke, huh?" she said to Jerry.

"Mom, I just got here," he said. "Can't you even say hi to me?"

Jerry didn't stick around the farm to visit very long last night. He talked Dennis into going back uptown, down to the Bible camp to hang out. I'm sure he didn't even come home last night, or he would have gotten everybody up by trying to cook a hamburger or scrambled eggs.

My mother tells me I'd better finish eating my toast because Mrs. Sheehy said she would be by the farm early because it's a long drive to Camp Buckskin. Mrs. Sheehy is our new social worker. When my mother spots a car turning off the highway, she says, "That's probably her. Where's your box?"

"It's right there, by the door," I say. But it's not Mrs. Sheehy coming down the dirt road. The car just keeps going past the farm.

I sit by the big picture window and watch. It's still pretty dark out. Normally Mrs. Sheehy's car is easy to spot. It's a shiny brown, almost-orange color. She usually sends a letter letting my mother know what day and time she's going to stop by for a visit to see how things are going. My father always goes to the barn or garage. He doesn't like social workers. Dennis says they remind him of what a lousy job he's doing in providing for his family.

My mother comes to the dining room table with a cup of coffee and her *McCall's* magazine. One of her sisters sent her a subscription for her birthday last year. She asks me why I'm looking at her and not watching for Mrs. Sheehy.

"Are you still gonna be visiting Frankie and your sisters when I get back from camp?" I ask.

"That check isn't here yet," she says, turning pages.

"But I heard Dennis telling you that if your check doesn't come by next week, he'll borrow you the bus money."

She shakes her head and tells me to keep my eyes on the window.

"I wouldn't care if you're still gone when I get home," I say. "I just don't want to be here alone with that Jerry. You know how he is. Just like it was in Milwaukee. He'll always be telling us we can't go upstairs with Dennis and him. He'll only cook just enough food for himself. And then he'll start stealing, too. Remember that time when he stole some of your money from washing dishes at the restaurant in Milwaukee?"

"You remember that?"

"Of course I do. Don't tell him about your Indian check, Mom."

My mother tells me I shouldn't be worrying about her. She says I'll forget all about this place once I get to Camp Buckskin. "And that's the way it should be. You're going to get your chance to learn how to swim just like Philly. And you'll have a lot of fun canoeing around the lake."

I can't stop staring at her while she reads her magazine and continues to talk about other things I'll get to do at camp. All of a sudden, I don't want to leave home. I want to stay with my mother. I want to go with her to Milwaukee, but I know there is no way she'll ever let me.

By the time Mrs. Sheehy finally arrives, it's light enough out to read the Koochiching County Family Services sign on the side of her car. I'm already standing in the driveway with my box when she opens her door. She's not wearing her normal work clothes—gray jacket and a white blouse. She wears pink shorts and tennis shoes with socks that barely touch her ankles. And her brown hair is not curled up on her head this morning. She has it pulled back behind her ears. She apologizes to my mother for being so late. "And we still have to pick up another kid in Mizpah before heading to camp. It's almost a four-hour drive to Ely."

She opens the trunk with her key and walks back to my mother. I stuff my box in the trunk and lean against the car, waiting.

Mrs. Sheehy waves at my mother. She jingles her keys at me and tells me to hurry and give my mother a big hug good-bye. My mother squeezes my shoulder and tells me to behave, to make sure I have a good time. She smiles just a little. "And don't you dare come home with an attitude. You hear me?"

I glare at my mother and pull away. I reach for the door handle, but suddenly I feel her hand touching mine. She slips some folded dollars between my fingers.

My mother stays in the driveway, staring at me as we leave. I look away from her. Whiskey barks as he runs along the side of the car. Mrs. Sheehy drives slow, saying she doesn't want to run over the dog. I tell her Whiskey chases after chip trucks and other eighteen-wheelers on the highway all the time. When we turn onto the dirt road, I look back to see if my mother has gone inside the house, but she is still there, watching me. I watch her, too, until the grass along the road gets higher, blurring her, fading her away from me. I tell Mrs. Sheehy that it's okay to speed up.

>[ ]<

During lunch, we don't see Tex or Brian. Cabin members are required to eat together at the same table. Nobody says anything because we think we know that Brian probably started another fight with Tex. I'm not sure if I like Brian or not. He compliments me on my drawing, and he thinks I'm very good at playing field hockey. But Brian acts like a big shot in our cabin. If he didn't have red hair, I'd say he looked just like my brother Jerry—always worried about getting his clothes wrinkled, always holding his cologne up by the light to see if anyone's been using it.

When they excuse us from the dining hall, our counselor, Gil, tells us not to go back to the cabin. Like always, we're supposed to have "R and R" time for a half hour in our cabins after lunch to read or write letters. But Gil says we have to go and hang out at the boat-house until our afternoon sessions begin.

As I put the tub of dirty dishes from our table on the stainless steel counter, Gil comes up to me. He asks if I would go back to the cabin and help Tex pack his things.

Tex is not his real name. His name is Douglas. We call him Tex only because he wears cowboy boots all the time, even during field hockey and canoeing.

I became one of Tex's only friends the first day I arrived. I couldn't untie the twine around my box of clothes. He pulled out a Swiss knife. I knew Tex would have a hard time getting along with other campers because of the way he dresses. He looks nothing like someone named Tex. Even though we're the same age, he's a lot shorter than me. He has a blonde buzz cut on the back of his head and long bangs that he keeps pushing aside. But it was his clothes that made me believe he was going to get picked on. All of his shirts are button-down, short-sleeved rummage-sale shirts I would wear at home but never at school.

When I get inside the cabin, Tex is folding his shirts neatly and placing them in his ripped suitcase that's almost bigger than he is. There's a bruise on his cheek. He turns away and wipes his eyes. I stay by the door.

"Do you want me to help you?" I ask.

He says nothing.

Once he turns back to his folding, I can't help notice that he buttoned his shirt wrong again. It's crooked. I tell myself not to say anything about it, but I do. I don't want everyone laughing at him when I help him carry his suitcase to the parking lot.

He mumbles and nods, then fixes his shirt.

The first time we had arts and crafts, Tex and I finished gluing together our popsicle-stick birdhouses early. The art counselor wanted us to go to the dining hall and flatten some little cereal boxes because she was stapling them to her cabin wall. In the huge kitchen pantry, Tex looked around at all of the shelves of canned fruit and said he and his younger brother never get fruit cocktail at home. He asked me if I hated being poor like his family. Then he started laughing, saying how embarrassing it was to go grocery shopping with his aunt. He wishes they never would have invented food stamps. Then he asked me if they make all the students who get free lunch stand in a separate line like they do at his school. He told me one of the best things about Camp Buckskin (besides the food!) was no lunch tickets. When I flattened an empty box of Rice Krispies, Tex asked me if my mother ever buys us Frosted Flakes or Honeycomb, that he only gets to eat Honeycomb when he and his brother go to the foster home when the county takes them away from their aunt once they find out she's been drinking nonstop for a week. I looked at Tex and told him he needed to straighten out his collar. And then I told him he shouldn't be telling people he's poor and living on food stamps with his aunt. I told him other campers wouldn't understand. They'd only make fun of him.

But since that day in the pantry, things have been bad for Tex. It was Brian. At first it was only the teasing, then it was the shoving and tripping. Last week was the first time Brian slugged Tex in the gut, making him lose his breath.

I look up and see Tex trying to close his suitcase. I don't bother asking him if he needs my help. I hold down the lid as tight as I can until I hear him snapping it shut. Tex slowly sits down on his bed while pushing his bangs across his sweaty forehead.

In between breaths, he asks me if I'm going to the all-camp dance tonight. For the past few days, Tex has been asking me if I was planning on going, and if I wasn't, would I want to catch night crawlers with flashlights.

"No, I'm not going," I say. "I can't dance."

I help him lift the suitcase from the bed and to the front door. He reaches in his back pocket and pulls out his chain wallet. He asks if I have a pen. I go to my bunk bed shelf and grab a Flair pen that I use for drawing.

Tex takes out a small piece of paper from his wallet and asks if he can still write me like we agreed we would when camp was over. He scribbles down his address and folds it. I slip it under my drawing paper on the shelf.

"He's going to pay for this, Tex," I say.

"Don't start anything with Brian," he says. "Just forget about it. I will." He smiles. "I'm looking forward to going back to being Douglas again."

I stand in the gravel parking lot, watching the Camp Buckskin van disappear down the road that curves through the woods. When the big bell rings, I start running back to the cabin to get dressed in my gym shorts for field hockey. I won't be playing on Brian's team today. Our rec counselor told us yesterday that he would be splitting us up because it's not fair to the other team. I think it's a good idea, too, putting Brian and me on opposite teams. I think it's a very good idea.

When I reach the field, I see Brian holding two hockey sticks, one in each hand. Our eyes meet, and I slow down, turn toward the equipment shed.

"Hey, man!" he yells. "I saved your stick for you!"

He follows me, catches up just as I sit on the bench with a pair of cleats. "Is it going to be a good game today?" he asks as he sits next to me, still holding my stick. And then he puts his hand on my shoulder and smiles. "I got a cool shirt for you to wear to the dance tonight."

"I don't know if I'm going," I say, lacing up my cleats.

"Man, you have to go! That Liz chick is. She's telling everyone about you!"

I suddenly feel my face turning hotter than the sun. I didn't think anyone knew about Liz. We don't hang around together that much, not enough for anyone to think I like her in that way.

Brian lowers his voice and hangs his head down. "Listen, man. I'd like to say he had it coming. That little shit really did get on my nerves. But I know I got a temper. You should see the way I whale on my little brother."

I hear the whistle blowing. I take my stick from Brian. I stand up, and he puts his hand on my elbow. "You're gonna love this shirt, man. It's got these far-out rhinestone cufflinks. I was going to wear it tonight, but I want you to. I think it'll look better on you." He holds up two fingers making the peace sign. "So, what do you say?"

I stare at his face. He's not smiling anymore as he waits for me to answer him. I give him a peace sign, and we run out to the middle of the field.

>[ ]<

It's after eleven o'clock by the time we get back to the cabin. Brian and I were the last ones to leave the dance. I waited for him while he argued with one of the counselors, wanting to know why we couldn't keep the dance going until midnight.

Brian switches on the lights and slaps the sides of bunk beds, yelling at everyone to get up. "The party is only starting!"

But not everyone is asleep. Osgood, a kid who looks at you sideways when he's not wearing his thick glasses, is pressing his face against the window screen. He asks Brian if he wouldn't mind keeping it down.

Brian grabs a towel and snaps it against Osgood's bare back. "Whatcha doing there, Osgoodie?" Brian says, laughing. "Wishing on a girlie star?"

When I start taking off the shirt Brian let me wear, I see an envelope on my pillow. Sometimes mail doesn't get delivered until night. I guess sorting out mail for nearly two hundred campers is a big job. I haven't received any letters from home in the two weeks I've been at Camp Buckskin.

"I'm listening," Osgood says to Brian. "Do you mind?"

I pick up the envelope and read the return address: The Rolo Family. Box 142. Big Falls, Minn. 56627. I can tell by the perfect handwriting that the letter is from my sister, Philly. It feels like there are at least five pages inside.

"Oh, yeah, Osgoodie?" Brian says. "You listening to the crickets? You think they're talking to you? I know! It's a wolf! You're listening to a wolf barking at the moon!"

Brian starts howling, getting some of the other guys to do the same.

I tear open the envelope, but I don't pull out my sister's letter. I know what it probably says. Philly will write about my mother leaving for her visit to Milwaukee, how she rode along to the bus station in Bemidji and begged my mother one more time if she could go with her. She'll write to me about the old man drinking more now that my mother is gone. She'll write about Jerry always making a mess in the kitchen, sleeping in until noon. She'll write to me about wishing she didn't have to watch Robert all day and night, and how sick she is of being the only one around the house who does all the cleaning and laundry. She will write to me that she wishes she could just run away and be with me at Camp Buckskin.

I turn and see Brian snapping his towel at Osgood while everyone continues to howl. I don't wonder what else Philly wrote about
home. I don't want to know, not tonight. I stick my sister's letter
on my shelf. I grab the painted pet rock I made in arts and crafts
and put it on the envelope, making sure to cover up the return
address. Then I stand up on my bed and howl louder than everyone
in the cabin.

⟨[18]⟩

Star Stick

The grasses of the farm fields are taller, but the pine trees along the side of the dirt road seem smaller. Mrs. Sheehy slows her car down as soon as she sees Whiskey racing toward us from around the corner of the house. The farmhouse looks more gray, even older.

When we turn into the driveway, I see a flat football and a tricycle with the front wheel twisted. I think my father must have run it over when he came home drunk some night.

My father stands by the side of the garage with the lawn mower on its side. His hat is on sideways, and he has grease stains on his overhauls.

Mrs. Sheehy honks her horn as we reach the end of the driveway. I point to my father, who walks toward the car, then I jump out and fall on the grass with Whiskey. I look up at the grimy kitchen window and wonder if anyone else is home. My father rubs his hands on the sides of his pants. He walks to Mrs. Sheehy, who is still in the car, leaning her arm out the window. My father laughs a little and says he would greet her with a handshake, but he gets pretty stingy with his oil.

"Oh! Don't worry about that!" she says. "My boys have spent the entire summer in our garage working on an old Buick."

My father looks at me and asks if I enjoyed camp, if I learned how to tie a sailor's hitch. I don't know what that is, but I nod my head yes anyway.

When Mrs. Sheehy starts telling my father that I must have had a great time at Camp Buckskin because I was so sad to leave, crying until we stopped for a cheeseburger and malt, I get up and decide to go inside.

"Now, where's Corrine?" Mrs. Sheehy asks.

I hear my father telling her that my mother has not been feeling well since she got back from her trip to Milwaukee.

I see only John when I get inside the old house. He's in the living room on the couch. He barely says hi to me because he's glued to the TV, watching one of those British comedies. The dining room table is cluttered with Pepsi bottles and empty bags of Oreo cookies and cardboard pizza boxes. I ask John who bought all the food. And then I have to ask him again, louder this time.

"The old lady got her Indian check last week," he says, still staring at the TV. "There isn't a lot left, though. The check wasn't as big as she thought it would be, and she had to pay Dennis back for her trip to Milwaukee."

I go into the kitchen to see if there's any of that pop left in the refrigerator. I glance out the window and see my father taking my box of camp clothes out of the trunk. I open the last Pepsi. I pick up a letter off the table. It's written to my father. My mother sent it to him when she was in Milwaukee. I skip the first few lines about my mother asking how things are going at the farm, if Philly was taking time to help Robert learn to walk. She asks if Jerry found work. I turn to the second page.

. . . *I went over to Sylvia's for supper on the second night. When Frankie dropped me off, I made him promise to come back and get me after he got off his shift. As much as I was excited to see my sisters, I didn't want to spend a sleepless night with them and their drinking. All their goofy laughing and arguing.*

Frankie took us bowling last night. Well, I didn't bowl, but Germaine did. That Germaine looks more gorgeous than ever. She just glows all the time. She can't wait until the wedding in December. Frankie said he's been saving a little from each check for me. He wants me to come back down here for the December wedding, but I don't know . . .

John calls for me, and I wait a few seconds just so he knows I'm not gonna be bossed around anymore. I slowly walk into the living room, sipping my pop. "Make it quick," I say to him. "I'm gonna ask Mrs. Sheehy if she can drop me off uptown."

He keeps his eyes on the TV and hands me a bottle of milk of magnesia. "Will you take that to the old lady?"

"Why don't you do it?"

"I'm watching this show."

"Well, do it when the next commercial comes on."

John calls me a shithead and jumps up from the couch. He snatches the blue bottle from me and storms off.

"How come you're going upstairs?" I ask.

"Because the old lady's upstairs."

"Why isn't she in her bedroom?"

I put my Pepsi down on the dining room table next to the other empty bottles and follow my brother.

The upstairs is hotter than the rest of the house. I think if my mother is feeling better, I should ask if she has enough Indian money left for an air conditioner.

I look past John. The bedroom door at the end of the hall is open. I can see my mother on her side.

I stand in the doorway, not saying anything. The fan is blowing on my sleeping mother. She's not wearing any socks or shoes. I stare at the burn scars wrapped around her legs. She mumbles something to John as he holds out her bottle of milk of magnesia. She keeps her eyes closed as she reaches for it, trying to sit up. John whispers that he forgot to get a spoon. She shakes her head, and he opens the bottle for her. My mother takes a small gulp and hands it back to him. Then she opens her eyes. "Where's the baby?" she whispers.

John softly says Robert is still napping in her bedroom downstairs.

She tells him to let her sleep a little while longer and when the baby wakes up to bring him upstairs.

John leaves the bottle on the floor where she can reach it. He nods at me to leave with him. I let him pass by me, then look back at my mother. There's a large spot of dried blood on the sheet underneath her.

I stand at the bottom of the stairs and hear Mrs. Sheehy's car starting. Whiskey is barking.

"I thought you were going uptown," John says.

"I decided I want to walk."

>[ ]<

After doing my last dive off the channel bridge, I swim to the rocks and tell Mike Hovan that I should probably be heading back home. I spent the night at his place and most of the afternoon swimming. The channel is the deepest part of the Big Fork. It splits off from the river about a quarter of a mile from the Bible camp. Years ago, the channel was created, and a concrete dam was built for a new power plant. But the plant stopped running sometime before we moved to Big Falls. I didn't go near the channel last summer because I couldn't swim.

"You're not staying over?" Mike says. "Frickin' school starts on Monday. This is our last free weekend."

"I can't," I say. "Are you done with that towel?"

He hands me the towel, and I dry my face and arms.

"I thought we were going back to Melissa's?" he asks.

"Mike, she doesn't want to mess around with you or me."

He pulls his T-shirt over his head, then reaches for his Marlboros and lighter sitting next to his wallet on the ground. "I don't know what got into her," he says. "She was horny as hell all summer. I swear. She couldn't get enough of me."

"I think you're lying," I say to him. He doesn't say a word because he knows the closest he ever got to messing around with Melissa Russell was squeezing her boobs on the playground.

"I gotta get home," I say as I start toward the highway. Mike follows and keeps asking me to stay another night. I don't want to say "my mom" is probably mad at me for being gone so long. Instead, I say "the old lady" is gonna be pissed if I don't get back.

Mike walks his bike with me up the hill until we get to Hagen's Corner Bar. When he sees his dad's pickup parked in front of the bar, he asks if I want to play some pinball and have his dad order us some fries. I don't get a chance to tell him I really have to get home because I spot Philly waving good-bye to her friend Jackie. Philly is about a block down the highway. I yell at her to wait up.

My sister and I walk along the train tracks. We stop once in a while to skip stones across the swamp between the tracks and Highway 71. Philly asks me what cabin I stayed in at camp. She asks if I liked Duffy and Nancy, the people who run Camp Buckskin. I just shrug and tell her I never said much to them, that I was too busy hanging out with my friends. "You didn't learn to smoke, did you?"

she asks. "Last year the older kids used to smoke down by the beach at night." And then she asked me if I met anyone that I liked.

"Her name is Liz," I say. "I got her address. She lives in Hibbing."

About a quarter of a mile away from town, I spot a skinny red tube about a foot long on the tracks. I show it to Philly, asking her what she thinks it could be.

"I have no idea. There's some writing on it, but the ink is rubbed off."

My sister shrugs and says we should probably leave it, that probably someone from the railroad company will come looking for it. But I tell her I want to show it to John. He'll know what it is.

She reaches for another stone but does not get a chance to skip it across the swamp. We see my father's Oldsmobile coming down the highway, pulling to the edge of the road. My mother is in the front seat with her head hanging out the window, and Dennis is in the backseat. Jerry gets out of the driver's seat and yells that they have to get Mom to the emergency room in Littlefork.

I yell back that we can't get to the road because of the swamp. Philly takes off. She splashes through a shallow part. I stay and watch her running up to my mother.

My mother leans her head more out the window. I look closer. Her eyes are closed and her arms are folded, probably holding her stomach. She cries loud in pain, a sound I never heard from her before. I look away, but I can still hear my mother's crying as if I were standing right next to her. There are no other cars on the highway, but it feels like someone is listening—the entire forest hears, listening closely to my mother's crying pain.

Philly wants to get in the car, but Jerry tells her she has to watch Robert. My mother screams again. "Hurry!" The Oldsmobile speeds off, kicking up gravel from the side of the highway. Philly watches for a long time, just stands there looking down the highway. I stare at the quiet swamp. The swamp waters stop rippling as the wind dies down. The forest gets darker. I call for Philly to come home. We have to watch Robert.

✢［ ｝✢

Scott, Michael, and I collect sticks from under the willow tree in the backyard for the campfire. I told my brothers that I was pretty good at starting a fire by rubbing sticks together. But when we get back to the pit, I don't have to try and prove it. John comes down the back porch steps with the stick I found on the train tracks. The tip is lit up, glowing bright red.

We sit around the fire and take turns holding the stick. John keeps telling us to point it down, not up, or we'll get burned.

My father told Philly and me what happened with my mother when we got home. "For the past three days, I had a hell of a time trying to get your mother to go to the hospital. And then she started bleeding more, screaming in pain. I could hear her clear out to the garage. I told Jerry to drive her to Littlefork. I had nothing but grease all over my clothes. I don't know what's wrong with her. She might have to stay in the hospital for a long time. I'll drive up and see her tomorrow."

Philly comes outside, saying she can't stay out too long because Robert is just barely asleep. John hands her the stick. Philly's face shines bright red when she holds it close. She says we need to start being nicer, to stop thinking so much about ourselves. "We need to do more things for Mom when she comes home. I know when I'm old enough to get a summer job, the first thing I'm going to do is buy that dress for Mom."

"What dress?" John asks.

"It's pink with violet flowers."

I tell Philly and my brothers that when I get a job, I'm going to do the same.

"You're not even eleven yet," Scott says. "You won't even turn eleven until December."

Philly hands me the stick, and I stare into the glow until I see spots when I look away. I ask John if we can put it out and light it again tomorrow night. But he says no. He wants to show me why. We all watch as he stabs it in the dirt, covering the flame. He waits, then pulls it out. It's still glowing. Even when he dips it in a pail of water, it won't go out.

"That's what a flare is," he says. "You can never put it out."

We head out to the field and throw the stick into the night as high as we can fling it, watching it streak back down like a falling star. I look up at the real stars. They look even brighter than most nights. It's impossible to believe they won't burn forever. But one day, they too will streak back to the Earth. I just hope it's not tonight.

❧ 19 ❧

The Smile of Whiskey

Jerry is standing on the dirt road in front of the farmhouse, waiting for Scott and me. We missed the bus because we stayed after school to play flag football.

I can't imagine what he's going to say. He is not grinning, snapping his fingers, or flexing his arm muscles like he does just before he starts teasing us.

When we get close enough, Jerry puts his hands in his back pockets and stares at the dirt. He says it only once. I laugh and tell him to come up with a better joke. He turns to the house, crossing the path through the dry ditch. I laugh again and tell him he's full of shit.

It only becomes more real when I see Philly running toward me with tears pouring down her red cheeks.

She grabs me by the shoulders and tells me they're lying, all of them, including John. She pulls on my sleeve, dragging me to the house. She begs me to go upstairs and tell them to just stop it once and for all.

I believe a little more when I get to the kitchen. My father is sitting at the table with his legs crossed, his head down, ashes dripping from the rolled cigarette between his fingers. Empty Pabst beer bottles line the table, sparkling in sunlight.

And I almost believe it really is true when I see Hank Cloutier standing by the stove with his hands folded, agreeing with my father—"Yes, yes, she was a very good woman."

But the truth twists back into a lie when my sister stops crying and wipes her face with the dish towel. She tells me she told them that she wants to see her. My sister buttons her coat and says she wants me to go upstairs and ask someone to drive. She wants to see her right now.

I leap up the stairs, thinking I'm going to tell Jerry that I want to go see her, too. But I stop and grip the railing when I see the door of her bedroom at the end of the hall is closed. I hear whispers coming from another bedroom. I walk slowly down the hall to see John and Joseph staring out the window, looking across the fields. Dennis and Jerry sit in chairs, their elbows on their knees holding their faces, looking at the bare wood floor. Whiskey stares at me with his big brown eyes, panting, smiling like he does when we're all together.

Dennis looks at me. I ask why her bedroom door is closed. He looks down again, and I do the same. I begin to believe again.

Whiskey follows me as I walk down the stairs, holding the railing all the way to the bottom.

My sister is not in the kitchen. I quickly race out the back door. I stop running when I get close enough to be sure she's not in the backseat, making sure she's not waiting inside my father's Oldsmobile.

I think about asking Hank Cloutier if he would drive into town. Maybe they called back, talked to Irene, told her it was a false alarm. But when I get back inside, Hank asks if I am hungry. He points to a glass pan covered in tinfoil sitting on the stove. He says Irene made a casserole for us.

Hank doesn't wait for me to tell him "no thanks, I'm not hungry." He steps to the table with a paper bag and fills it with my father's empty beer bottles.

I stand in the dining room and watch Scott and Michael. They are on the couch, curled up, their hands covering their eyes, their sobs trying to rock their bodies to sleep.

In the bedroom, my sister shares a pillow with Robert, holding his tiny hand in hers. He giggles and kicks his feet. She kisses him, then wipes her tears from his forehead.

It finally becomes the absolute truth when I sit on the broken front porch steps and feel the hot flood of my own tears melting my eyes and face.

When I see his feet, my brother standing next to the lilac bush, I tell him to go away. He tells me he has something that will make me feel better, something that will stop the hurting. I tell him again to go away. But he stands there until I look up at him. He's not grinning or flexing his muscles. So I ask him what he wants to give me. He sits down beside me and holds a small, dark brown bottle in his hands. He twists off the cap and says it will taste awful, but he promises if I take two big swigs, it will make the pain go away. But I can't get past the smell when I bring the bottle to my mouth. I give it back.

Jerry stays until Whiskey comes and sits with me on the broken porch. I listen to the dog's panting, then look at his smiling. He sniffs the warm breeze as he watches the road. I put my arm around him and pull his head to my chest. I hold his face to mine, staring into his brown eyes. I want to tell him he should stop waiting. But then I think maybe it's not entirely true, maybe he should watch and wait. I let him go and he sits up. I rub his back and stare at him, watching his smiling at the road.

⟩[20]⟨

Eyes in the Sun

I always make sure I am the first one up to help Germaine in the kitchen. Sometimes, like this morning, I even get up before she does. I pull out the iron frying pan from inside the oven and place it on the stove burner. I make sure there's plenty of matches, and I make sure the spatula is clean. I open the refrigerator to see that we're out of eggs. I grab the ice cream bucket and head out to the chicken coop.

Frankie and Germaine got on the Greyhound bus together the day after my mother died of a heart attack during her operation. My father says she had a lot of internal bleeding. He called Irene Cloutier from the Littlefork hospital that morning and told her my mother's heart just gave out. The doctor and nurses couldn't do anything for her. They couldn't bring her back. She was forty-six years old.

Frankie would have driven up in his convertible, but he told my father it never would have made it to Duluth. Frankie plans on staying with us for a few more days after the funeral. He would like to paint the kitchen a nice yellow color. He says when the aunts arrive, he's going to ask if they have enough room in their car for Germaine. She has to get back to her job at the shoe store in Milwaukee.

I wish Germaine would stay as long as Frankie. We like the food she cooks. I didn't think I would like Germaine's tuna hotdish with melted cheese because I never had it before. My mother never made tuna hotdish. She was like me. We hated the taste of fish.

Once I get outside and see the bus roaring down the dirt road, I realize that I had almost forgotten about school. The bus doesn't stop, hasn't stopped since the day after my mother's operation.

We're down to just a handful of chickens now. The rooster and most of the hens were butchered last winter. I wish that rooster would have lived longer. I'm sure I wouldn't hesitate in clobbering him with my bucket. Sure of it.

When I get back with the eggs, Germaine is pacing around the kitchen, brushing her light brown hair. She's wearing her high-heeled boots and short leather jacket because she can't take the cold mornings. She smiles and asks me why I didn't wake her up sooner. She says she's embarrassed by sleeping in.

I don't think Germaine has ever been this far away from the city. She stands back with her hand in front of her face while I light the stove for her. She really thinks if she tried lighting it, the whole house would explode.

I stand next to her at the stove and watch her flip the eggs. I ask her if she likes the ring that Frankie bought her. She turns her hand and looks at it. "It's a pretty small rock," she says, laughing. "You're brother's such a cheapskate."

"I wish we could go to your wedding," I say.

"Ah, there's so many of you guys," she says. "I don't know where you would all sleep. Frankie was going to get your mother a motel room because he didn't want her staying in his apartment alone."

Suddenly it gets silent like it sometimes does since my mother's death. Sometimes in the middle of playing football, my brothers and I will stop bragging or even fighting over the score. We keep playing, but we don't say a word. We heard that silence last night while passing around the photographs that Germaine took of us making faces at the camera, laughing and shoving each other.

But it goes away when Germaine switches the subject, when she asks us if she can cut our hair, if we would like to go shopping for some new clothes. The silence goes away because Germaine doesn't say how much she misses my mother. She doesn't tell us that she wishes my mother would have lived long enough to see Frankie get married.

"Will you show me where the Laundromat is today?" she asks when I hold out a plate for her fried eggs.

"I didn't know you knew how to drive."

"Ah, I can drive, just not on the freeway." Suddenly Germaine puts her hands on her hips and smiles at me. "Hey. You know, you sound just like your brother. I'm a very good driver. Frankie just doesn't know it."

>[ ]<

My mother's sisters picked up James at the bus station in Duluth. Aunt Sylvia steps behind James's dining room chair and yanks his long, black hair. "We thought he was a girl," she says, laughing with the other sisters sitting around the table, eating some of the chicken they ordered for everyone. When my aunts got into town late this afternoon, they bought two bags of chicken from Strickler's Café.

And then Aunt Sylvia starts in on Frankie, remembering the time when he tried growing out his curly hair and sideburns, trying to look like Tom Jones.

"It would have worked," Aunt Victoria says. "But poor Frankie can't sing or dance!"

But the laughter of my mother's sisters finally quiets down. I stare at their brown, round arms, thinking how they look just like my mother's. They wear bright red lipstick and use an eyebrow pencil like my mother. The only difference is what they wear— new red and green dresses, gold flowers and silver birds pinned on their chests, shiny high-heeled shoes and nylon stockings with no holes.

When it gets late, I wonder if my mother's sisters are going to drive up to the bar and buy some beer. Or maybe they already have some in their station wagon. But they don't have beer tonight. Tomorrow we have to go to the funeral home in Littlefork for the wake. The day after that, we'll go to St. Joseph's Church uptown for the funeral. Irene Cloutier told my father that the ladies in the church will prepare a lunch in the basement of the community hall.

The aunts scoot their chairs back and say even though they spent one night in a motel, it sure was a long drive to Big Falls. My father tells them that Germaine and Philly put clean sheets on my mother's bed, and he set up a cot he borrowed from Merle Mac.

By the time I get downstairs, I can smell coffee. My aunts are already up. They sit at the dining room table with my father. Aunt Philomena, the youngest of my mother's sisters, has her pointy glasses on. She's writing something down on a notepad. I sit at the kitchen table and listen.

"We bought some nice dresses before we left, Don," Aunt Philomena says. "You can choose the one you think Corrine would like."

"No, that's fine," he says. "I went to Penney's with the lady from the funeral parlor earlier this week. She looked for the dress that Corrine had her eye on for quite some time. It's not the exact same one, but I think Corrine would like it."

"What about her hair? You know Corrine liked her hair a certain way."

"Well, I showed the lady the few pictures I keep in my milk can. I said there was some hair dye at home that Corrine never used. I told her I look at that box every day. It's sitting there on the windowsill. But the lady said not to worry. She said she would take care of it. Before I left, she looked through the pictures again and said Corrine was beautiful, a very beautiful woman."

>[ ]<

When it's Philly's turn to get her hair cut, she tells Germaine to just trim her bangs. But Germaine takes more time with Philly. She asks my sister about her favorite subjects in school (math), if she would like to move away from Big Falls one day, and if she's thinking about going to college when she's ready.

I look at the clock on the kitchen wall and say it's almost 5:30. I sit in the dining room, wearing the new jeans Frankie and Germaine bought me, waiting for everyone.

My father comes out of the bathroom, buttoning his new white shirt. He shaved and combed his hair back. Germaine asks if he has a tie. And he says no, that the last tie he ever wore was on the day he got married. I think about that black and white photograph of my mother at her wedding, how she was staring off somewhere while everyone was laughing and having a good time. I look out the big picture window like my mother used to. I think I had seen that same look in her eyes a thousand times since we moved to Big Falls.

When it's time to leave, nobody knows where Dennis is. Joseph checks the barn, and John goes out to the dirt road and calls for him, thinking he might have gone for a walk. Dennis does that once in a while, more since our mother died.

But we can't wait. Frankie, James, Jerry, and the aunts will meet us at the funeral home in Littlefork. They wanted to cross the bridge into Canada, drive around Fort Frances. "It's our only chance," Frankie says, laughing. "A once-in-a-lifetime experience."

Germaine did not want to go. She is sure Canada is even colder than Big Falls. She spent most of the day with Philly, trying to figure out what my sister would want to wear to the wake.

Germaine and Philly sit in the front seat with Robert. The rest of us pile in the back of my father's Oldsmobile. Whiskey chases after us, of course. I lean out the window and tell Whiskey that he can't go because they won't let him. They won't let him see her.

When we turn off Highway 71 to Littlefork, I end up thinking about what my mother looks like in the casket, something I promised myself I wouldn't do. I have to look into the falling sun. Staring into the sun explains why there are tears in my eyes in case anyone asks me what's wrong. The crying should have ended by now after that first morning when I was so glad the bus never stopped and honked for us. I knew I couldn't stop crying long enough to wave the driver away. On the farm, I can go off and be alone without worrying if anyone is looking. So when I'm trapped around everyone, I stare into the sun.

But there's no sun in the funeral home. All I can do is bite the inside of my mouth or press the tips of my fingers together as hard as I can to keep the crying away. And I think this works because there are no tears blurring the gray casket at the front of the room. There is no blurring while waiting in line with my sister and brothers to see my mother for the first time since that day she went to the hospital. My eyes are clear when I look at my mother's sleeping face, her thick black hair, thin eyebrows and red lipstick, her new pink dress with purple flowers. Maybe the crying has left me for good, finally. But for the first time since that long day after my mother's death, when I turn to go back to my seat, the tears return nonstop when I see my aunts' faces. I don't care if anyone sees my tears now. I don't need to wish I could stare into the sun because I see the same tears in the eyes of my mother's sisters.

⟨21⟩

Ghosts that Dream

The laughter of my aunts returns after the morning funeral. When we come back to the farmhouse, the sisters gather around the dining room table and pass around beers. They light their Winstons. They start with teasing my father. Aunt Sylvia wonders how he's going to get along now without an Indian woman around to raise hell with him, keep him in line.

The dark clouds and drizzle make it seem later than it is. But no one turns on the dining room light. Scott and I lean over the couch and look at my aunts and my father sitting in shadows with their cigarette tips glowing. But I hear the silence again after Aunt Sylvia suddenly turns serious. She tells my father he should sell this old farm and move back to Milwaukee.

My father puts out his Winston and takes a drink of his Pabst. "I got a spot right next to Corrine when it's my turn to go," he says.

My mother's sisters will be leaving tomorrow. Germaine will go with the aunts. Frankie plans on staying for a few more days.

Germaine stands by the back door and calls for Scott and me. She wears her leather jacket and holds her Instamatic camera. She has a few more pictures left but no flashbulbs. We stand in the rain in our bare feet, pulling our sleeves down past our hands, trying to stay warm in the rain. Germaine tells us to just stand still for a few more seconds.

"Are your aunts telling stories about your mother, about growing up at Bad River?" she asks.

"No, I haven't heard any," I say, trying not to move. "I thought that's what you're supposed to do, tell funny stories."

Germaine takes the last picture. She shrugs and says they will tell those stories when they're ready.

We follow her upstairs and sit on the bed while she packs the camera in her denim bag. She sits between Scott and me and tells us to make sure we study hard and to keep helping out around the house. "I appreciate your hard work this past week," she says, smiling. "I sure wish I could train that Frankie to pick up after himself without having to be told all the time."

"You really can't stay longer?" I ask her. "Not even for a couple more days?"

"I'll get fired," she says. "Besides, I kind of miss the shoe store. It'll be good to get back to work and make some money for the wedding." We hear the silence again, and Germaine says she can't wait to get those pictures developed. She promises to mail them to us. But the silence remains this time, so Germaine lightly slaps my knee. "Listen, you guys," she says. "It's going to be better once you go back to school. It really will. Every day will be a little bit easier."

>[ ]<

My father is alone now at the dining room table in the darkness. He strikes a match, lighting a butt. The aunts have already gone to bed. They plan on leaving before it gets light out.

Whiskey scratches at the back door. I don't want to turn on the light to find my shoes. I want my father to go to bed.

I watch the dog sniffing around the wet grass in moonlight. I think about having to go back to school on Monday. I want to go to school again at Lincoln Elementary in Milwaukee. I want to leave with Germaine and my mother's sisters in the morning.

When we come back inside, the dining room is empty. Whiskey goes upstairs to sleep with Joseph. I curl up on the couch and use my coat for a pillow. I close my eyes and plan to get up before my aunts. I try thinking about getting out the frying pan for them, lighting the stove so they can have some eggs. But my mind begins drifting, and it's hard to think about other things I want to do in the morning for my aunts. The room turns pitch black, and I feel myself slipping into that darkness, that sleep.

Suddenly I hear the squeaky oven door opening in the darkness. Someone is shoving pans inside. I sit up and see the kitchen light is on. And then I smell her bread.

I stand up but can't feel my feet touching the wood floor. I see myself floating toward the kitchen. I place my hand against the dining room wall, afraid I'm going to fall. When I get closer to the kitchen, I see shadows swaying—my mother's dress. I look around the corner and Whiskey's tail wagging. My heart is jabbing hard against my chest.

I close my eyes again, then float close enough to see her leaning against the sink, eating a piece of her bread smothered in melting margarine. I see the loose threads and grease stains on her green dress. My mother's hair is not made up, and it's streaked with gray. I watch her hand as she lowers it to Whiskey, sharing her bread. I see the snakes, the burn scars wrapped around my mother's legs.

"Do you want some bread?" she says, cutting the loaf. "It's nice and warm."

I can feel the linoleum floor now as I step into the kitchen light.
I ask if she had a chance to talk to her sisters. She shakes her head
and smiles. "Good Lord, no! You can't get a word in edgewise when
they get going. Here, take your bread."

"Did they tell stories about you?" I ask. "Growing up in
Odanah?"

"Sure, but they weren't as funny as the one they told about the
time I packed up the house and moved to Big Falls with all you kids."

"Don't forget the old man," I say.

She points her bread knife at me, glaring. "He's not the old man.
He's your father. You hear me?"

"You call him that."

"What did I tell you about bringing home an attitude?" I don't
answer my mother. She asks if I had a good time and enjoyed myself
at camp, if I made a lot of friends. I don't answer her. She pours a
cup of coffee at the stove, then sits at the table. She tells me to take
the dog out because she wants to get started on a letter to Frankie.
I don't move. She reaches for a small cardboard box. It has a pink lid
and purple flowers. She opens the box and takes out a clean white
sheet of paper, no notebook lines or ripped edges.

Whiskey scratches at the door. My mother asks why I am still
standing in the kitchen, if I'm hard of hearing.

"I want to stay with you," I say.

She sighs, then reaches for an empty chair, sliding it close to her.
"If you don't want to take the dog out, then go get your math workbook. Mrs. Mattson says you're missing five assignments."

"But I'm not in the fourth grade anymore," I say. "Mr. Reese. He's
my fifth grade teacher."

"You better get that workbook. Mrs. Mattson says if you keep
falling behind, she'll have to hold you back a year. And there won't

be anything I can do about it because I won't be around forever. You'll just have to learn the hard way, on your own. Now, go get it. It's on the table in the other room."

I float to the dining room table. I look around the empty beer bottles and ashtrays, but I don't see the math workbook. I almost yell back to my mother that I can't find it when I spot some photographs of Scott and me, the pictures Germaine took of us standing in the rain. I smile when I see our faces cringing in the cold. I pick them up to show my mother. But the kitchen light is now off. I wonder why she wants to sit in the dark. I flip the light switch on, but Whiskey is gone and my mother's gray casket is in the middle of the room.

I feel my legs jerk, and I quickly open my eyes. The house is quiet again. And when I look to the kitchen, it is just as dark as it was before I drifted off.

>[ ]<

I realize Germaine and my aunts might already be gone when I get up. The dining room table is wiped clean. A white vase with red flowers is the only thing on the table. I go into the kitchen to look out the window to make sure their station wagon is gone from the driveway. But I don't have to do that to be sure. There's a letter to my father on the table.

Don,

Thanks for putting us up the past few nights. It was good to see you and the boys, and Philly. We all thought the services were very nice. Please tell the ladies at the church thanks again for the thoughtful meal they prepared for us. Corrine looked beautiful. We'll be praying she has a safe and peaceful journey now.

We nearly forgot about the groceries in the back of Sylvia's wagon. You should cook up that roast today. I put it on the top shelf in the

refrigerator. Just preheat the oven to 350. Cut up some carrots, onions,
and potatoes along with the meat and cover it. Let it cook for about an
hour and a half. There's a couple loaves of bread we bought sitting out
on the counter.

Take care and please write us. Let me know how things go, especially
with Philly. I couldn't get over how much she looks like her mother.

Love,

Philomena

I put the letter down and think how much my aunt writes just like
my mother.

I go back into the living room and fall back to sleep on the couch.
When I wake up, I see my father at the dining room table, drinking
more beer in the sun that's shining through the big picture window.

Frankie comes out of the bathroom, and I ask him if he knows
what time it is. He tells me it's a little after ten. He puts on his sweat
jacket and asks if I want to drive into town with him to buy some
paint at the hardware store.

During the ride, Frankie says nothing about the aunts visiting
or the funeral. He talks about getting a new car and driving back
up to Big Falls next summer. "I want to see Mom's grave," he says.
"I'm hoping Dad will be able to save up enough from his monthly
check to buy a gravestone or some kind of plaque."

"He could if he didn't drink so much," I say.

Frankie does not say anything. I don't think he liked what I said
about the old man drinking too much. I don't think he likes me calling our father the old man, either.

He parks my father's Oldsmobile across the street from the hardware store, and we get out. We can see our breath. "Shit, it's colder
than I thought," he says. He blows into the air and watches his
breath float away.

I ask him why he wants to paint the kitchen for Dad.

"Well, it won't improve the value of the house much, but it will make it more attractive for potential buyers. I told Dad there's no reason to live this far north." And then he looks at me. "You know, Germaine and I will be starting our own family in the next few years. I told Dad we want him to see his grandchildren more than once a year."

When we get home with the paint, I see James shredding carrots at the sink. The old man is still drinking. He takes a beer out of the refrigerator and tells James he should cook up the roast. "You can't rely on your mother anymore," he says, stumbling back into the dining room. "She's gone now."

Suddenly James rushes past me into the dining room. I hear the old man's beer bottle smashing. I run into the dining room and see James grabbing another bottle off the table. He whips it across the room and tells the old man he wishes to God it would have been him who died.

Suddenly James starts shoving the old man in the back, making him spill the tobacco he's trying to pour into his cigarette paper. Frankie throws down his bag of paintbrushes on the kitchen table and goes after James, slamming him to the floor. James doesn't fight back. He just screams at my father, blaming him for forcing my mother to move up to this godforsaken town, not giving a damn about how lonely she was, how that loneliness killed her, and how it was all his selfish fault.

Jerry and Dennis come running down the stairs. They have to drag Frankie out of the dining room, pushing him through the back door, down the porch steps.

James slowly gets up and pulls his messy hair back. He punches the wall as he goes to the front bedroom. I stare at the old man.

"I loved your mother," he mumbles to himself, wiping his eyes with the backs of his fists. "I really did. I really loved that woman."

But I don't know if I believe him. I don't know if I should ever believe my dad or not.

>[ ]<

As I drift off to sleep, watching the room turn pitch black again, I suddenly feel Philly pulling at me, telling me that we're home. "It's time to get off the bus." I look around and see that it's now light out. I am on the school bus, not on the couch. As I float up the driveway, the air feels so hot, I have to take off my coat. I wonder how it got so warm out, why I don't see my breath.

When I get to the house, the back door to the kitchen is wide open. I see her again, sitting at the table smoking a cigarette. She wears the long, black wool coat that she bought at the Salvation Army. Her hair is all black and pretty, just like the way the funeral parlor lady fixed it. I don't ask her why she's smoking. Sometimes when she is in a really good mood, listening to James's Carole King music, she asks him to let her have a few puffs, that she just wants to hold it like Elizabeth Taylor.

I ask her why she has her coat buttoned all the way up to her neck. She does not hear me. I look at the other end of the table and see James peeling potatoes, swaying his head to the Carole King song coming from the radio on top of the refrigerator.

I tell James it's way too loud. He does not hear me. I grab the cord of the radio and yank it from the wall. James laughs at me and gets up, going to the stove. A cloud of black smoke pours out of the oven when he opens the door.

"Now look what I've done!" he says to me. "I burnt the damn bread!" He grabs the dish towel. He yanks out a pan of black bread and whips it across the kitchen against the yellow painted walls.

"I'll never be able to bake bread," he says to her. "I gotta get off this farm! I can't stay here and cook for these papooses." He storms into the dining room without saying another word.

I look back at her. She takes her arms out of her coat sleeves. She is wearing the pink dress with purple flowers.

"Go to the store and buy another package of yeast," she says, putting the cigarette out in a saucer. "When you get back, I want you to start in on a new batch of bread."

"I don't know how to bake your bread," I say.

"Well, you better start learning," she says. "You can't rely on me anymore. I'm leaving."

I turn off the oven and close the door. "Why do I have to be the one to cook now? And don't say it's because I'm not a baby anymore. Don't tell me I have to start acting my age. Don't tell me I will be eleven in December."

She buttons her wool coat again, all the way up to her neck. She folds her arms and rocks a little in her chair as if she's trying to stay warm. "I'm not going to tell you how to do anything. Why should I? You never listen to me. So I'll put it to you this way. Either you walk to town and get some yeast or you're all going to go hungry when it gets cold this winter."

She fades into darkness. It suddenly feels chilly. I blink my eyes open, then look around the living room. I reach down to my feet and find my blanket. I pull it up to my chin and wait until the room gets lighter from the big picture window. When I can see my breath above me, I squeeze myself as close to the couch as I can. I close my eyes and drift off again.

>[ ]<

Before he leaves, Frankie finds my younger brothers and me in the front bedroom downstairs. The first day back to school was easy, like Germaine said it would be. No one, especially Mr. Reese, asked me if I was okay, if I still cry when I get to missing my mother as bad as I do.

Frankie leans against the gray wall and looks around the room that used to be my mother's. He thinks a coat of light blue would look nice. He wishes he could stay and paint all the rooms. But he has to go. He has to get back to Milwaukee and Germaine.

Jerry and James left this morning. Frankie offered to drive them to Bemidji in the Oldsmobile, but Jerry said it would be easier hitching a ride with one of the truckers uptown when they stop at the gas station. They didn't want to stay another day with the old man.

Dennis didn't go to school this morning. When I went out to the barn after I got off the bus, the only thing I could think to ask him was why he wasn't excited to see his girlfriend, Angie. He told me he's quitting school. He said he is going to stay with his friend Dale Olson for awhile so he can figure out how to get the hell out of Big Falls for good.

Frankie opens his wallet and pulls out a ten-dollar bill. He tells me it will be my job to split it up fairly with Scott and Michael.

"What about Robert?" I ask. "We should buy something for him."

Frankie runs his fingers through his curly black hair. "Well, that's the other thing I wanted to talk to you guys about," he says. "Dad has to start cutting wood for the winter. There will be no one here to watch Robert. That friend of Mom's . . ."

"Irene Cloutier," Scott says.

"Yeah, I guess she offered to babysit, but you know Dad can't afford to pay anything. And he's too proud to tell people that."

"So what's he going to do with Robert?" I ask.

Frankie tells us he's going to live in a foster home. Mrs. Sheehy came by the farm today to make the arrangements. She told our father she would have the county start the paperwork.

We never saw Frankie cry before or after my mother's funeral. And he's not crying now, but he has tears in his eyes. I ask him when he's leaving. Hank and Irene are giving him a ride to Bemidji to catch his bus. They have to take him tonight. The bus leaves at five in the morning. Frankie will have to sleep at the station.

Before he says good-bye, he forces us to hug him—Scott, Michael, and me. Then he hugs Philly.

He walks to the garage where my father is showing Hank the used chainsaw he bought. We lean close to Irene's window, daring her to tickle us. But she only smiles. "You boys be good while we're gone. You be real good and mind your dad. Will you do that for me?"

Once Frankie and the Cloutiers leave, I tell Philly I can wash the supper dishes by myself, so she can give Robert a bath before he goes down for the night. My father is still in the garage. I decide to sleep with Scott in Dennis's empty bed. I don't want to sleep on the couch again. I know it will be just like the other nights. She will find me, my mother.

I go upstairs with a pile of folded clothes. Scott and Michael are running, jumping on the bed. I tell them to quit roughhousing and to pick out which shirts and pants they want to wear for school tomorrow. I tell them to make sure they put their lunch tickets in the pockets of the pants before going to bed.

When my father finally comes in from the garage, it's past ten-thirty. He scrubs his hands in the sink and asks where the older brothers are. I tell him they all went to town to stay over at Dale Olson's—Dennis, Joseph, and John. He says nothing. I offer to make him a hamburger. He says that's okay, then asks me to get the liverwurst. He opens a bread bag and says it's late.

I tell my father I should take Whiskey out one more time. And while I slip on my shoes, I notice my mother's hair dye is still on the windowsill. I don't ask my father why he never put that hair dye in the basement, in the box filled with her bread pans and her wool coat.

Whiskey follows me to the edge of the yard. The fields are quiet. A few days ago, a flock of wild geese landed in our fields. But they're gone now, back on their long journey.

I look at the farmhouse. The upstairs is dark. I call Whiskey and tell him it's time to go to bed. I decide to turn on the light in the bedroom, leave it on all night.

When I open my eyes, the sun is already up. I look around the room and listen for any footsteps in the hall. And when I'm sure she is not here, not waiting for me anywhere in the house, I realize it's safe to get out of bed.

I quickly dress because I know the school bus will be here soon. I tap on Scott's shoulder and tell him it's time to get up. I do the same to Philly when I go to her bedroom. In the kitchen, I fill a pan with water and light the stove. I look at the clock on the wall and yell upstairs that the bus will be here in twenty minutes. I set out some clean bowls and spoons. When the oatmeal is cooked, I turn off the stove. I go to the bottom of the stairs and yell for my brothers and sister to get moving. "The bus will be here soon, and your oatmeal is getting cold."

›[22]‹

My Mother Is Now Earth

My father comes through the back door into the kitchen with a big round metal tub. He tells me we have to start melting snow so we can do the laundry. "The well is going dry. I'll put this on the grate, and you boys get some buckets and fill them with snow."

I take a bite of the last piece of yellow cake I made for my birthday, then slip on my boots. I couldn't make any frosting because we can't afford to buy powdered sugar.

I call for Scott, who is watching curling on TV. He says he'll help me later, after it's over. I want to tell him he's just lazy, that no one in the house likes curling. "Let's go, Scott," I say. "It's going to take all night to melt enough snow for just one load." Scott asks for five more minutes, and I go back into the kitchen.

I look at the wedding pictures Frankie and Germaine sent us. My brothers and I passed them around while my father read Germaine's letter out loud. Frankie is now making plans to continue on with college. Germaine says he can get a better-paying job with a four-year degree than just the certificate he got at the technical school. They're moving to Oshkosh. Frankie wants to get a business degree at the University of Wisconsin campus there. And Germaine says the used white Dodge that Frankie bought is running great.

They're going to drive up next summer to visit us and Robert and Philly.

My sister moved into the same foster home as Robert just before Thanksgiving. My father didn't argue with Philly when she wanted to leave. He told Mrs. Sheehy that his daughter would be a young woman soon. He said he could handle taking care of the three younger boys.

I have to get after Scott to turn off the TV and help me with the snow. I know Michael will eat the last piece of birthday cake, so I stick it in my coat pocket.

It doesn't take us long to finish getting bundled up now that we don't have to look for a decent pair of gloves. Dennis had to take his with him when he moved out, when he hitchhiked to Minneapolis. But Joseph and John let us have their gloves when Mrs. Sheehy drove them to the group home in the Falls. My father didn't argue with my brothers about leaving, either. He told Mrs. Sheehy that he had no control when it came to trying to get them to go to school and church.

When Scott and I get outside, it's warmer than we thought it would be. It's been so cold for the past few weeks. My father says too cold to even snow. We can still see chicken blood in the old snow. A few weekends ago, my father and Merle Mac butchered more hens. They would have killed all of them, but all of a sudden something got into Whiskey. When he saw Merle carrying a hen by its legs to the chopping block, he started barking in a high-pitched voice like he was in pain. And then he went after Merle. Whiskey bit into his overhauls and wouldn't let go until Merle dropped the hen. My father told Merle they'd better call it quits for the day.

Once we get the tub filled with snow, I ask Scott if he wants to go back outside and play catch with the football. But my father pulls out a handful of change and spreads it on the dining room table. He says he's getting low on tobacco, and would we be willing to walk uptown to buy him a can of Prince Albert before the Red Owl closes? My father's Oldsmobile does not have enough gas to make it there and back. He says if we do that for him, we can have what's left of the change, and he'll take over filling the buckets with snow.

We wait for him to write the note for the cashier. His note is the only way we can buy his tobacco.

Whiskey races ahead of us on the dirt road. Once we reach the highway, we cross over to the railroad tracks. We always take the tracks when the dog comes with us since he almost got killed by an eighteen-wheeler during deer hunting season. Whiskey got too close to that truck. Scott says he tried biting one of the back wheels. He went spinning and flipping to the other side of the highway until he slammed into a snowbank. Whiskey was curled up, shaking and panting. He couldn't move, and we didn't want to hurt him more by trying to carry him home. Then a pickup stopped and a hunter got out. He took one look at Whiskey and said his back was broken. The hunter pointed to his truck at a rifle hanging in the back window. He said it was the only thing we could do for him. But we said no.

He helped us lift Whiskey into the front seat of his truck. Scott and I hopped in the back, and the hunter drove us to the farm. There was hardly any snow on the ground, so he roared his truck right up to the back porch. He got out and helped us bring Whiskey inside.

We laid our dog on a pile of blankets in the kitchen corner and took turns sitting with him, gently holding his front paw and lightly stroking his face. My father thawed an extra pound of hamburger. He fed it to Whiskey while we were in school. But only a few days after getting hit by the eighteen-wheeler, our dog was up on his feet.

I give my father's tobacco note to Mae, who's working at the Red Owl register today. Once she puts the Prince Albert in a small paper bag, Scott and I head to the candy aisle with the change. I see an Indian man standing at the meat counter. I tell Scott he looks like the same Indian who came by the house last June. I can't be sure because he's wearing an overcoat. I can't see his huge muscles. The Indian who came by our house had bigger arm muscles than Jerry. But when he checks the time on his watch and I see that black leather band with blue, red, and yellow beads sewed on it, I am sure it's the same Indian.

We don't know if we should say hi or not. Not even Scott can remember his name.

But I don't think he ever told us who he was. All we knew about him was that he used to be in Vietnam and he liked to put out his cigarette on his tongue. But what we remember most about him is what he did with another cigarette. He tore it open and put some tobacco in his hand. He went outside in a rainstorm and placed the tobacco in a small hole in the willow tree in our backyard. A few minutes after he got back inside, the rain stopped and the wind died down. An hour later, we could see the sunset.

He came to our farm because my father got to talking to him at the bar, of course. My mother was surprised to see my father coming back so early. But that Indian told my mother they heard on the radio at the bar that there were tornadoes in the area.

We never asked him what it was that he did with the tobacco. My mother used to tell us to make sure never to ask an Indian when they do those kinds of things.

The first time I heard her say that was right after we moved to Big Falls. We were still living in the garage at the time. My mother was baking her bread and telling Dennis a story about when she and her sisters moved to Milwaukee after the war was over. Her sister

Victoria ended up in the hospital with a certain kind of cancer on her face. Some old Indians came down from Odanah to see Aunt Victoria. They said Chippewa prayers for my aunt, then rubbed some kind of plant mix on her face. I can't remember how many days later it was, but my mother said when the doctors examined my aunt, they couldn't find any trace of the cancer.

But that Indian remembers our names when he sees us. He winks and asks us if our crazy white father is behaving himself. Scott blurts out that he drinks only on the first day of the month now. Then he sobers up because he has to buy groceries. He's afraid Mrs. Sheehy will come by and find there's nothing to eat in the refrigerator. Scott never stutters once while saying all of that to the Indian.

And then the Indian asks how our mother is doing.

"She died in September," I say. "She had a heart attack on the operating table."

The Indian stares right into my eyes and whispers, "Your mother is passed on, not dead."

He remembers Whiskey's name, too. The Indian kneels down on the icy sidewalk outside the Red Owl and shakes our dog's front paw. He takes his big hand and gently touches Whiskey's panting face. Then he slowly moves his large hand down across Whiskey's crooked back.

Scott and I can only shrug when the Indian looks up at us. I tell him Whiskey doesn't act like he's in pain, and he runs just as fast as he did before he got hit by that eighteen-wheeler.

The Indian stands up and puts his hands in his overcoat pockets, his package of meat under his arm. He stares at me in the eyes again. "Your mother must really love this dog."

Scott and I are silent. We look at Whiskey, who is smiling. "You boys keep that in mind, now," the Indian says. "You keep that in mind wherever you go. Never forget it."

I ask him if he's going to stop by the farm to see my father. But he says he has to be leaving. His ride's waiting for him at the bar. He doesn't know when he'll be coming through this way again. But if he does, he will be sure to see us.

When we get to the railroad tracks, Whiskey begins to bark at us. At first we ignore him, but he keeps barking. And then he starts jumping and running around, still barking.

Scott and I look around, wondering if maybe a wolf is following us in the woods, even though we've never seen one before. I tell Scott that maybe we should hurry fast. As soon as we start running, Whiskey stops barking. It's hard to run in winter boots. We don't get very far before we have to stop and take a break. But when we do, Whiskey barks at us again. So we run some more and we stop again, hoping the wolf has given up on us. But he must be still following because Whiskey barks and keeps barking until we run again. It's like this all the way to the dirt road leading to the farm. It's about another quarter of a mile. I look back at the railroad tracks and the woods while Whiskey barks nonstop. I tell Scott I think we're okay because we're out in the open.

Scott tries to calm Whiskey down by petting him, but our dog won't quit. Light snow begins to fall as we walk, as Whiskey barks on. Suddenly the snow gets thicker and the wind picks up. We can barely see the farm.

We try running again, but we just can't do it anymore. And so we walk, trudge through the blinding snow, listening, following the sound of Whiskey's bark the rest of the way home.

>[ ]<

I hang the last shirt on the clothesline between the dining and living rooms, above the iron grate. My father sealed off most of the house to save heat. He laid a blanket on the bottom of the closed door leading to the upstairs. We're not allowed up there until spring. He doesn't mind if we go into the downstairs bedrooms, but the doors have to stay closed at all times. But we don't go in those rooms very much. He removed the beds. He set up his bed in the dining room and the double-wide in the living room. My brothers and I take turns sleeping with Whiskey on the couch and bed.

My father sits at the kitchen table with his milk can at his side. In between sorting through papers and old photographs, he is working on a letter to Germaine. I slice a piece of cheese for Michael. He asks if there is any more bread because he doesn't like the heels. My father says he bought six loaves of bread on the first. He can't believe they're all gone, and it's not even the middle of the month yet.

Michael sits at the table with his cheese sandwich and asks if we have to melt snow to take a bath, too. My father says there's water if we use only enough to get wet. I sit on the other end of the table and sort my own papers in my math folder. Michael picks up some photographs and slides them toward me. I nod and glance at the black and white photograph of my mother's wedding day, how she stares off, looking past everyone, her eyes drifting.

My father asks if I have any homework. I tell him no. I'll have to ask Mr. Reese for help because I can't figure out how to multiply fractions.

"Then would you like to read what I wrote to Germaine?" he says, holding his letter out to me. "Read it to yourself and tell me what you think, if there's anything else I should add."

I take my time skimming through the letter . . . *I bought a twenty-pound turkey for Christmas. I wish I knew how to bake bread the way Corrine did. Bread is getting expensive these days . . . thinking of raising some pigs next spring. I'm thinking maybe four sows and a boar . . . got a good routine going now. I make a batch of chili with macaroni and corn during the week and pancakes on Saturday night. The boys and I play rummy. Mrs. Sheehy, the social worker, says there's a speech camp down toward the Twin Cities for Scott to go to next summer . . . I'm thinking seriously about selling off the farm in a few years when I make the last payment. I really should be closer to the Cities the older I get. They got a veterans hospital down there. Of course, I hate to leave Corrine. But I can't stay here forever, especially after the boys get older and graduate from high school. I don't know what I would do all by myself in this big old house and farm . . .*

I put the letter down on the table and wait for Michael to leave after he's finished his sandwich. And then I look at my father. "I think your letter is fine."

"You sure?" my father asks. "Maybe I shouldn't write anything about wanting to sell the farm."

"No, it's fine," I say, picking it up and giving it back to him. "It's a really good letter, Dad."

>[ ]<

I must have slept through the entire night because when I hear the sound of Whiskey's panting close to my face, I open my eyes and can see him in the morning light. Whiskey is waiting for me to get up from the couch. My father is snoring in his bed in the dining room. I look at the big picture window and see snow falling.

I go into the kitchen. It's almost seven o'clock. I put on my coat and stick my bare feet in my boots. I open the back door and follow Whiskey outside.

The new snow sparkles when streaks of sun peek through the clouds. An early winter morning is as quiet as it gets on the farm and in the forests across the dirt road. But over by the willow tree, I hear footsteps crunching through the snow. I see someone in the tree's shadow. I look at Whiskey. His ears rise and his tail straightens.

But he doesn't bark, and I don't step backward to the porch steps. I see her. Whiskey runs and leaps through the snow, his tail wagging. I trace his tracks to get to her, my mother.

She is picking up some twigs that have fallen from the willow tree, stuffing them in her long wool coat. She bends down and takes the dog in her arms. I kneel and scratch behind Whiskey's ears. I see her bare legs. The bronze snakes that wrapped their skins around my mother for so many years are now gone.

"I'm only back to get a few things I will need," my mother says, reaching for another twig. "Some kindling for the fires. I was hoping to find a little food."

I remember the birthday cake I hid in my coat pocket. I take it out and give it to her.

"That bear is out there," she says, looking across the dark fields. "He keeps his distance, though." She puts the cake in her coat pocket. "I always like to leave him a little something after I put out my fires when I'm ready to move on."

My mother reaches down and gently strokes Whiskey's back. She says she will not be coming through this way again. She looks at me in the eyes and says I shouldn't fear that bear when he finds me at night.

I don't ask what she means.

My mother pulls her coat close to her body and smiles, just a little. She stares off, looking past me, her eyes drifting. I turn, wanting to know what my mother sees. But the new snow is falling thick now. I can't see where the tops of pines disappear into the rising sky. I can't see where the fields end and the forests begin.

AFTERWORD

July 15, 2011

The burnt-out farmhouse is long gone, torn down years ago. The barn is gone as well. But the garage we moved into during that bitterly cold spring of 1971 still stands. My dog, Rock, sniffs around a patch of grass, and I think about looking through one of the windows. But I don't. I know she is not there. I know the flow of years has entirely eroded away my mother's presence from this place.

The mosquitoes on the farm are thicker than I remember growing up. I call Rock to my side, and we walk a little faster across the yard, past the lilac bushes that used to guard the broken-down cement porch. We stand near the sprawling swamp willow and stare across the fields leading to the line of pines that have grown taller now. After my mother passed on, we stayed here for five more years, my two younger brothers and my father. We helped him fulfill his dream of making the farm work. We baled hay, raised pigs, and grew acres of potatoes each summer. During ancient winter nights, we eased my father's loneliness by popping corn and playing cards with him.

But the poverty and the drinking never ceased. When my father's rage erupted, whether he was sober or drunk, I was the target— blamed for his sins, accused of being "just like your mother." I never said a word. I continued to get my brothers up for school, make sure they had clean clothes, and speak to their teachers about missing homework.

But I was defenseless in my dreams. Many nights, the bear found me standing in an open field. I raced back to the house, reaching the steps of the porch only to feel his claws pulling me down, his teeth tearing into my flesh. I knew that charging bear would harass my imagination as long as I lived on that farm. I struggled terribly with my own grades in school, but I was determined to be like my older brother Frankie and go to college.

Though I was older now, my father insisted I make my First Communion at St. Joseph's Catholic Church. We did not go to Mass every Sunday, but when we did, my father made sure we arrived early enough so he could go to confession. My brothers and I could only imagine what sins he dared ask the priest to forgive.

Some mornings, after attending services, my father drove us out to the cemetery. He did not mind my younger brothers staying in the car, but he expected me to walk with him to her grave. I waited as he knelt down and whispered to my mother. As he stood, always with his face turned from me, he would point to the spot next to his wife's grave and remind me that's where he was going to be buried.

When my father made the last payment on the land in December 1977, he immediately put the eighty acres up for sale. We moved the following summer and pursued his new dream of living on the wooded shore of a lake near the Twin Cities. I hated the new high school and moved back to Big Falls, where I graduated, but he never returned to Big Falls, not even to be buried. During my freshman year at the University of Minnesota, I visited my father at the Minneapolis veterans hospital, where he was being treated for prostate cancer. As the cancer progressed, he decided he needed to be near his mother and sisters. He died in 1989 and was buried in his hometown of Antigo, Wisconsin.

I take one last look at the forest and fields of the old farm, then reach down to stroke the warm, black back of my dog. He pants, smiles in the burning sun, waiting for me. He stays at my side as we head down the driveway to the car parked on the side of the dirt county road. Rock is a Cane Corso. Roman soldiers trained his ancestors to fight alongside them during wartime. And they used his breed to hunt bears.

>[ ]<

Outside the old Red Owl grocery store, I lean against the car and peel the wrapping from a stick of beef jerky for Rock. I look across the street through the sweltering waves of sunlight at the Big Falls post office. My mother probably spent more time in that brick building than she did in the store or in the corner bar waiting while my father had "just one more."

My mother often edited her letters before taking them to the post office. She wrote first drafts, then did revisions on new sheets of paper. My father plucked some of those early drafts from the garbage when my mother was not looking. He kept them in his milk can with his other papers and photographs. I read and reread those letters, even when I returned home from college to visit my father. But when the cancer began to ravage his mind, those letters were lost.

While I have always regretted not snatching those letters from the milk can, I also know that for some of my siblings, the loss of physical memory has been a hidden blessing. When you grow up in such dire poverty and dysfunction, gaining distance from tangible reminders of the past—especially your mother's oppression—becomes critical to survival.

It took me years to get through college, to create my own distance, to find my own path. I ended up working full time as a journalist for *The Circle,* a Native American newspaper in Minneapolis. I always thought my mother would be proud that her son was advocating for American Indians, chronicling the ongoing struggle of our people. Writing about Indian people, bringing these stories into the public light, took the sting out of my mother's memory for me. Through the voices and faces of Indians, especially women, I gained a better understanding of my mother's own struggle—how she must have fought to stay strong, to endure for the sake of her children. The narrative of my mother's memory began to take on a new thread, a story of her survival that revealed more dignity than despair. I embraced the realization that it was inaccurate, even terribly unfair, to simply say, "My mother had a very hard life, and I can only hope she is in a better place."

>[ ]<

Rock Roy Rolo is actually my nephew's dog. I had hoped Nicholas would come with us to northern Minnesota to see the old farm, be charmed as I was by the quiet of a little logging town, marvel at the river and rapids that flow along the northern edge of Big Falls. But summers are short, coveted seasons when you are young. I'm sure Nicholas did not want to waste a perfectly good weekend hanging out with an uncle who is obsessed with traveling down memory lanes of gravel.

Rock and I are greeted by another swarm of mosquitoes as soon as we step out of the car at the Big Falls campground. Except for a young couple rolling up their tent, the park is empty. I hold Rock's leash, and we roam where his nose takes us. We walk between light and darkness casting down from towering northern white pines. We stare into the twirl of the roaring river, watching it crash against jagged rocks. We feel the breeze of clouds touching down, parting the heat around us. We stand in the presence of the Earth.

I had no intention of writing about my mother. Besides the reality that I was still a boy when she left us, my mother was extremely elusive. Not even my older brothers or my father truly knew her. All of her sisters passed on years ago. And when my siblings and I talked about our past, about growing up in northern Minnesota, we did not always share the same memories of events. From a journalist's point of view, there was little record to go on. Given the subjective stories of each brother, sister, and relative, I was not at all interested in attempting to construct a collective memory of my mother.

I also knew that in order to tell my mother's story, I would have to tell my family's story as well. And I could not do that. Somewhere between shame and pride, my siblings have guarded their own share of our history.

My nephew Nicholas lived with me in Madison, Wisconsin, during his high school years. I taught at the university. My nephew never asked much about his grandmother. I tried to give him a familiarity of her through random stories. I don't believe I was able to push the narrative past "your grandmother had a very hard life, and you should hope she is in a better place."

But two years ago, on an early February afternoon, while I walked through a snow-covered garden, the memory of my mother came to me like a drifting scent in the breeze, swirling through the branches of a nearby cedar tree. I was drawn back to the day I learned she had passed on. But that autumn day of 1973 did not grip me with deep sadness, the burden of never seeing her again. I was looking at that day from a new angle, a distant view that seemed to suggest a new, untold story. I was suddenly more than curious about who my mother truly was in this life and beyond. The more I lingered in the garden, the more I began to wonder if the land held memory, kept stories. I visited that garden often, well into April. In trailing rabbit tracks, whispering back to the wind, and catching rain in my hands, I was gathering story, my mother's story.

>[ ]<

I have tried to be careful in writing about the last three years of my mother's life, as she warned me in that dream. I decided this could be a story told only from my own specific memories of my mother. I sorted through my memories as if they were photographs spread out on a dining room table. In my mind, I drew a narrative line that focused on my mother's final journey in this life. Those photographs, select memories, became the structure for the book. I endeavored to write only about real people and actual events that happened from 1971 to 1973. But of course, many memories, especially those of a boy's, slowly fade or come to an abrupt ending. I needed to reimagine dialogue based on situation and character, to rewrite those letters I knew so well. In order to fill in the lost pages of those three years, I had to finish scenes, staying true to my memories of the time. It may have been more of a courtesy than concern, but I changed nearly all the names of the people in this book.

And I decided I needed to see my mother again. I needed to return to her gravesite in Big Falls, Minnesota.

>[ ]<

Turning into the narrow dirt cemetery covered in pine shade, I regret not pressing my nephew harder about making this journey with me. I am actually apprehensive about seeing my mother's grave. My heart shifts from warm memory to the sober present. I am meeting someone I have not seen in over thirty-five years. The fear surprises me because during the white heat of writing this story, those days when the intense work burned away time, I felt my mother in the room. Her presence was sheer mystery, and I embraced it.

I tell Rock he has to stay in the car this time as I open the door. My mother, like other wives of military servicemen, is buried in the veterans section. There are no tombstones here, only plaques of stone and metal.

Suddenly I understand my fear. A number of years ago, while I was working at *The Circle,* I had a deep stirring within, the kind only the soul can hear. *Your mother's bones need to be removed from Big Falls and reburied at her tribal home in Odanah, Wisconsin. It is time for her to come home to her relatives.*

I shared that stirring with some of my brothers, and they agreed that yes, one day, when the moment presents itself, we should have our mother returned home. But as I move between the graves, I honestly do not know if that stirring came from my own runaway imagination or if in fact it was my mother becoming restless, perhaps even angry at having to be left here all alone.

I squeeze the pouch of tobacco in my hand and move between graves, looking for her plaque. When I find her grave, I look down and read the words my father wrote one winter evening for the engraver. My father spent hours searching for a handful of words that would honor his wife in a way he never could when she was with him. *Corrine Bennett, wife of Don Rolo. Born 1926, Odanah, Wisc. Died 1973, Big Falls, MN.*

Tobacco becomes sacred in the act of presenting it to our elders, to those who have passed on. The gift is a silent request to join hearts, minds, spirits, to be one with each other and with the Earth. I sense that my mother knows I have come here with trepidation. I am a boy again. I feel as if I have come home to a mother who has been waiting up for me, wondering where I have been all day, all summer, all of these years. But as I lean down to give her the tobacco, my mother says nothing about my long absence, nothing about any neglect or failings along my own journey. She only nudges my soul. *More dignity than despair.*

"Here, Mom," I whisper to her. "This is for you."